Notoriously Active—God in His World

Notoriously Active
—God in His World

Lenten Readings from William Stringfellow

Jeffrey A. Mackey

WIPF & STOCK · Eugene, Oregon

NOTORIOUSLY ACTIVE—GOD IN HIS WORLD
Lenten Readings from William Stringfellow

Copyright © 2020 Jeffrey A. Mackey. All rights reserved. Except for brief quotations in critical publications or reviews, no part of this book may be reproduced in any manner without prior written permission from the publisher. Write: Permissions, Wipf and Stock Publishers, 199 W. 8th Ave., Suite 3, Eugene, OR 97401.

Wipf & Stock
An Imprint of Wipf and Stock Publishers
199 W. 8th Ave., Suite 3
Eugene, OR 97401

www.wipfandstock.com

PAPERBACK ISBN: 978-1-7252-5599-9
HARDCOVER ISBN: 978-1-7252-5600-2
EBOOK ISBN: 978-1-7252-5601-9

All Scripture references are the editor's own translation.

"The Unity of the Church as a Witness of the Church," an earlier version of this work appeared in the *Anglican Theological Review* under the title "The Unity of the Church as a Witness of the Church" (vol. 100, no. 3, Summer 2018) and is used here by permission of the *Anglican Theological Review*.

Quotations from *Sojourners*, reprinted with permission from *Sojourners*, (800) 714-7474, www.sojo.net.

"Living with Defeat," in *The Witness*, May 1977. Courtesy of the Archives of the Episcopal Church.

"The Crisis Accepted," in *Youth in Crisis*, ed. Peter C. Moore (New York: Seabury, 1966). Courtesy of the Archives of the Episcopal Church.

"The Life of Worship and the Legal Profession," National Council, NYC, October 3, 1956. Courtesy of the Archives of the Episcopal Church.

"Through Dooms of Love," in *New Theology, No. 2*, edited by Martin E. Marty and Dean G. Peerman. Copyright © 1965 by The Macmillan Company. Reprinted with the permission of Scribner, a division of Simon & Schuster, Inc. All rights reserved.

Material from the following books by William Stringfellow used with permission of Wipf and Stock Publishers:

    An Ethic for Christians and Other Aliens in a Strange Land

    Conscience and Obedience

    Dissenter in a Great Society: A Christian View of America in Crisis

    Free in Obedience

    Imposters of God: Inquiries into Favorite Idols

    Instead of Death

    My People Is the Enemy: An Autobiographical Polemic

    A Private and Public Faith

    A Simplicity of Faith: My Experience in Mourning

    The Politics of Spirituality

https://prodigal.typepad.com/prodigal_kiwi/william_stringfellow/
—used under "Fair Use" policy.

Manufactured in the U.S.A.　　　　　　　　　　02/03/20

"Knowledge of the truth hidden in the first Advent, confession of Christ as Lord, means recognition of the sovereignty of the Word of God acting in history to restore dominion to humanity in creation." [1]

---

1. Stringfellow, *Conscience and Obedience*, 83.

Contents

Preface | ix

Ash Wednesday | 1
Thursday after Ash Wednesday | 4
Friday after Ash Wednesday | 7
Saturday after Ash Wednesday | 9
Monday after the First Sunday in Lent | 11
Tuesday after the First Sunday in Lent | 14
Wednesday after the First Sunday in Lent | 16
Thursday after the First Sunday in Lent | 19
Friday after the First Sunday in Lent | 23
Saturday after the First Sunday in Lent | 26
Monday after the Second Sunday in Lent | 30
Tuesday after the Second Sunday in Lent | 32
Wednesday after the Second Sunday in Lent | 35
Thursday after the Second Sunday in Lent | 38
Friday after the Second Sunday in Lent | 40
Saturday after the Second Sunday in Lent | 42
Monday after the Third Sunday in Lent | 45
Tuesday after the Third Sunday in Lent | 48
Wednesday after the Third Sunday in Lent | 51
Thursday after the Third Sunday in Lent | 53
Friday after the Third Sunday in Lent | 55
Saturday after the Third Sunday in Lent | 57
Monday after the Fourth Sunday in Lent | 60
Tuesday after the Fourth Sunday in Lent | 62

CONTENTS

Wednesday after the Fourth Sunday in Lent | 64
Thursday after the Fourth Sunday in Lent | 67
Friday after the Fourth Sunday in Lent | 70
Saturday after the Fourth Sunday in Lent | 72
Monday after the Fifth Sunday in Lent | 74
Tuesday after the Fifth Sunday in Lent | 76
Wednesday after the Fifth Sunday in Lent | 79
Thursday after the Fifth Sunday in Lent | 81
Friday after the Fifth Sunday in Lent | 83
Saturday after the Fifth Sunday in Lent | 85
Monday in Holy Week | 87
Tuesday in Holy Week | 90
Wednesday in Holy Week | 93
Maundy Thursday | 95
Good Friday | 98

Bibliography | 101

Preface

The celebrations of Advent, Christmas, and Epiphany are behind us and we enter, with the Incarnate Jesus into a Lenten labyrinth of anticipated and unknown twists, turns, and dead ends. It is interesting, that in the United States we do not post signs for "Dead Ends" any longer—they now read "No Outlet." It reminds one of Dante's "Abandon hope all ye who enter here." The implications of this change must be there, somewhere, but they are not captured by this editor's simple mind. William Stringfellow, Harvard-trained lawyer, Episcopalian, social activist, and social critic of the highest caliber, spoke and wrote much of the fall of humanity, its seeming, and actual "Dead Ends," and the recapitulation of all things in the work of God in Jesus Christ, the "Word of God." Though Stringfellow died several decades ago, his writings remain unquestionably pertinent to our life together in the twenty-first century.

The labyrinthine realities of life are addressed by Stringfellow in his reference to the God who is living and "notoriously active" in his world. Stringfellow would agree with Richard Swinburne that God has an obligation to his creatures, fallen though they be. "The best news of God is that He is no secret. The news of God embodied in Jesus Christ is that God is openly and notoriously active in the world."[1]

Though in the fall, "the reign of death is pervasive and militant,"[2] in the existence of time, "time itself is an aspect of fallen reality, a signal of the activity of death, (yes, the) most familiar and oppressive feature of the reign of death in the world."[3]

---

1. Stringfellow, *Private and Public Faith*, 17.
2. Stringfellow, *Conscience and Obedience*, 30.
3. Stringfellow, *Conscience and Obedience*, 28.

Nonetheless, "the Word of God is not somehow diminished or can not be confined, but still retains freedom from the parameters of time, embodies eternity in time, redeems time. To refer to the Word of God in temporal terms is always, therefore, quaint and stylistic, a manner of speaking, a metaphor, a parable."[4]

As Lenten wonderment ascends and descends upon us, and upon all the people of God, we are, by the writings of Stringfellow brought back, maybe even snatched back, for our own eternal benefit, to a place where we recognize that "the Word of God is for men [and women]. . . . The Bible has not merely relevance but, much more than that a present vitality of the Word of God for men [and women] in these times."[5] "The Word of God persists in fallen creation—inherent or residual, hidden or secreted, latent or discreet, mysterious or essential (cf. Romans 1:20; James 1:21). Having the eyes to behold that presence of the Word, or having the ears to listen to that Word, having the gift of discernment, is, indeed the most significant way in which Christians are distinguished from other human beings in this world."[6]

It is this discernment for which these writings are collected. Knowing that I, or no one, could sound the depths of Stringfellow's canon of work, I have, nonetheless spent over forty-six years reading and rereading all he has written, and found the profound experience that "the revelation of the Word of God is, always, more manifold and more versatile than human comprehension."[7]

In 1994, I was invited to be a fellow-in-residence at the School of Theology of the University of the South in Sewanee, Tennessee, with the express understanding that I research, discuss, and lecture on William Stringfellow. I came forth with immense amounts of materials of which I had not previous possessed and spent hours with active and retired faculty who had known Stringfellow personally. The wealth of information remains to be organized. This work is a mere scratching of the surface. Robert Boak

---

4. Stringfellow, *Conscience and Obedience*, 28.
5. Stringfellow, *Free in Obedience*, 7–8.
6. Stringfellow, *Conscience and Obedience*, 36.
7. Stringfellow, *Conscience and Obedience*, 11.

PREFACE

Slocum subsequently invited me to contribute an essay to *Prophet of Justice; Prophet of Life*, a collection of essays on Stringfellow, published by the Church Publishing Company.

So, it is to the Word of God, that Stringfellow will lead us during these forty days of Lent, beginning with Ash Wednesday and ending with Good Friday. It is my sincere hope as the editor that these subterranean fresh waters from Stringfellow's constant spring, will, in their unceasing artesian nature, fill and flood your mind and then your heart, to such an immeasurable depth, and will lift you to such immense vistas that your Lent will accomplish its purpose and your Easter will have a mat which most appropriately frames its glorious canvas.

The title, *Notoriously Active—God in His World*, is taken from *A Public and Private Faith*, where Stringfellow writes, "The news of God embodied in Jesus Christ is that God is openly and notoriously active in the world."[8] What more could motivate us to the keeping of a Holy Lent?

The prayers at the end of each day's reading are the work of the editor, along with some connecting commentary in several readings. These are *outside* the quotation marks which designate Stringfellow's own words. I have chosen to keep the generic "men," and "mankind," since this was Stringfellow's original. His capitalization or lack thereof has been maintained.

The editor's comments are of more length at the beginning and trail off as the reader becomes more and more familiar with Stringfellow's style. If you know his writings, you will need my editorial comments much less.

Jeffrey A. Mackey
Autumn 2019
St. Dominic's Chapel, Glen Alpine, North Carolina

---

8. Stringfellow, *Public and Private Faith*, 17.

Ash Wednesday

Anticipation is the commitment of the mind when approaching the Word of God. Lethargy is never enjoined; boredom is never an excuse; and hurriedness is never justifiable. The Word of God sets the Lenten example: time, rest, commitment, hope, wholeness—these are precisely the elements the cohesiveness of Lent anticipates. In looking into the Word of God, Stringfellow discovered that what he

> anticipate(s) in the passages is not consistency but coherence. I can live and act as a biblical person without the former, but not without the latter. . . . I look for style, not stereotype, for precedent not model, for parable, not propositions, for analogue, not aphorisms, for paradox, not syllogism, for signs, not statutes. The encounter with the biblical witness is empirical, as distinguished from scholastic, and it is confessional, rather than literalistic, in either case it, over and above any consideration, involves the common reader in affirming the historicity of the Word of God throughout the present age, in the biblical era and imminently.[1]

Ash Wednesday, yes, and all of Lent, must bring us face-to-face with the Word of God. If it fails to do this, we have been failed by Lent, and we have failed Lent. The Liturgy begins today with the Celebrant praying this collect:

> Almighty and everlasting God, you hate nothing you have made and forgive the sins of all who are penitent: Create and make in us new and contrite hearts, that we, worthily lamenting our sins and acknowledging our wretchedness, may obtain of you, the God of all mercy, perfect remission and forgiveness; through Jesus Christ

---

1. Stringfellow, *Conscience and Obedience*, 11.

our Lord, who lives and reigns with you and the Holy Spirit, one God, for ever and ever. *Amen.*

The service continues with the invitation to a *Holy Lent*:

> Dear People of God: The first Christians observed with great devotion the days of our Lord's passion and resurrection, and it became the custom of the Church to prepare for them by a season of penitence and fasting. This season of Lent provided a time in which converts to the faith were prepared for Holy Baptism. It was also a time when those who, because of notorious sins, had been separated from the body of the faithful were reconciled by penitence and forgiveness, and restored to the fellowship of the Church. Thereby, the whole congregation was put in mind of the message of pardon and absolution set forth in the *Gospel of our Savior*, and of the need which all Christians continually have to renew their repentance and faith.
>
> I invite you, therefore, in the name of the Church, to the observance of a holy Lent, by self-examination and repentance; by prayer, fasting, and self-denial; and by reading and meditating on God's holy Word. And, to make a right beginning of repentance, and as a mark of our mortal nature, let us now kneel before the Lord, our maker and redeemer.[2]

This Lenten invitation is to a life of spiritual simplicity in the presence of worldly difficulty since that which has been redeemed (the world) has not yet come to a complete comprehension and embracing of the real.

> The simplicity—not ease—but simplicity of the Christian life is founded upon the fact of the presence of the Word of God already in the common life of the world. The practice of the Christian life consists in the discernment of (the seeing and the hearing) and the reliance upon the (reckless and uncalculating dependence), and the celebration (the ready and spontaneous enjoyment)

---

2. *Book of Common Prayer*, 264–65.

of the presence of the Word of God in the common life of the world.[3]

Lord God, deliver me from ease into simplicity, from blindness to discernment, and from the safe into the reckless, that I become a Lenten person: a candidate for inevitable resurrection. Amen.

---

3. Stringfellow, *Private and Public Faith*, 56.

Thursday after Ash Wednesday

Lent inevitably draws us into the testimony of the Word of God concerning Christ Jesus. Lent is a time to "come close" and know *him* better. "The biblical witness is narrative, but not legislatively, it is normative in the sense that the Bible is the exemplary story of God's consistent and patient involvement in the history of mankind."[1] As we read the Bible, especially Lenten assigned readings, we are confronted again and again with the absolute presence of God in Christ working out the divine intent for the entire creation. The condition of creation at present, demands the hope and anticipation encapsulated in the Word of God. The general thought is that Christianity is a religion of some kind of Lenten dourness perpetuated to appease a wrathful God. Nothing is further from the truth. "In short, religion supposes that God is yet to be discovered; Christianity knows that God has already come among us."[2]

Lent exists, as does all of life, within the grace of God's self-giving. Lent is not dour it is life-giving; grace in action. We find ourselves not arguing for what we "give up," as much as proclaiming what God has *given!* Stringfellow captures this truth when he writes, "The truth of the Genesis creation story is not that God made human beings on the first Saturday, but that the life of the whole creation originates in the utterances of the Word of God. Life, since its inception, is a gift."[3]

This is prophetic. Life is a gift from the beginning. Do we hear this? Do we read this in the Law, the Prophets, the Psalms, even in the Gospels? No, legislation and legalism are, unfortunately

---

1. Stringfellow, *Second Birthday*, 43.
2. Stringfellow, *Private and Public Faith*, 16.
3. Stringfellow, *Conscience and Obedience*, 28–29.

the default for far too many believers. But such an approach to one's faith, the faith of the church, or even to the church's liturgics, misses the faith of the prophetic Word of God. "Prophetism is identified with the clash between the existence of the world and the presence of the Word of God in the world, and as well, with the tension between the life of the church at any given point and the Word of God whose presence in the world the church exists to hear, herald, and expose."[4]

As members of his church, we have a herald of something to hear and to then expose (evangelism). Lent falls into this exposition of the Word of God. Overt introspection is therefore, a borderline sin, if you will.

"Theology," writes Stringfellow, "is always in the first confessional,"[5] and therefore the Christian Lenten life is proclamation as well as confirmation in one's own life. It is not the type of moral doing which is to be our Lenten focus as if we could increase our sanctified state through self-effort, but rather, "it is the confession of the militance of the Word of God in this time and this place as much as consummately, which constitutes the mature ethical knowledge of biblical people."

Stringfellow reminds us during our Lenten journey, that

> the Gospel of Christ means the work of God in the world for the world [including you and me—added by editor]. Christ means the creative, comprehensive, specific, and conclusive concern of God for the common life and work of this world.
>
> When Christians overlook the Word of God, the peril is a disintegration of the Christian life in the world and an immobilization of the Christian mission for the world.[6]

The gospel is the empowerment of our Lent, not our own self-will. Try as we might we cannot match the power of the gospel.

---

4. Stringfellow, *Private and Public Faith*, 52.
5. Stringfellow, *Private and Public Faith*, 42.
6. Stringfellow, *Instead of Death*, 47.

Vain and fruitless is my struggle self to sanctify, therefore Jesus Christ, sanctify me that my Lent continue sanctified. Remind me of the gospel's power and my own lack of the same and aid my renewed decision to confess and proclaim that gospel. Amen.

The Friday after Ash Wednesday

We are not given the prerogative of judging or punishing others. Vengeance belongs to God alone, and when understood in the context of the Word of God, God's own forgiveness is indeed his punishment. If we, in forgiveness, pour "coals of fire" on our offender's head, how much more does God's forgiveness pile such coals of forgiveness on fallen humanity's heads? "Many men hate the Cross because it means a salvation not of their own choosing or making, but rather of God's grace and mercy. Men hate the Cross because it means salvation which is unearned, undeserved, unmerited. *Men would much prefer God to punish them than to forgive them because that would mean that God is dependent upon men and needed their obedience to be their God.*"[1]

As I write this in the summer of 2019, there is a raging racial divide in the United States. Stringfellow anticipated this for the same was true when he was ministering in Harlem decades ago. He prophetically captured the essence of our need for racial acknowledgment and forgiveness when he said, "The racial crisis had more to do with the meaning of Christ for men than all of these programs and pronouncements and conferences and committees."[2]

That renewal of the church is found in each of us taking ownership fresh and new of our baptismal vows. "Baptism is the assurance—accepted, enacted, verified, and represented by Christians—of the unity of all *men* in Christ."[3] We must be revisited by the arresting fact that "theology is concerned with the application of the Word of God in the world's common life."[4] Therefore the

---

1. Stringfellow, *Conscience and Obedience*, 33.
2. Stringfellow, *Conscience and Obedience*, 97.
3. Stringfellow, *Instead of Death*, 56.
4. Stringfellow, *Second Birthday*, 21.

current race question is addressed for it is common life; involved is offence, evil, vengeance, unforgiveness, and more. That is why when God sees these manifestations of the fall, he punishes by forgiving. The Bible tells me so is the testimony.

> It is the correspondence between biblical faith and empirical reality—or to say it somewhat differently—discernment of the militance of the Word of God incarnate in common history—which is the genius of the biblical witness.[5]

And in the Lenten journey it is incumbent on us to see ourselves, our *self*, if you will—possibly to rediscover that which makes us human persons like every other human person who ever lived, lives, or ever will live. I am not excused from the pervasive effects of the fall nor am I excluded by some arbitrary fiat of a fickle deity from the full provisions of salvation.

> The discovery of self, or, more precisely, the recovery of self—the gift of personal identity—is at the same time, the very theme of the Gospel. Christ is, preeminently, the man who knows what it is to be a human being. They do not know who they are as persons for the very reason that they have not yet recognized who He is.[6]

I stand guilty before the gospel, before the Word of God. There is no excuse except that I have been trying the self-redemption route and it is a dead end. The coals of fire on my head are more than I can bear; I accept your gift of grace and its mental and spiritual coolness. Thank you. Amen.

---

5. Stringfellow, *Conscience and Obedience*, 67.
6. Stringfellow, *Instead of Death*, 24.

Saturday after Ash Wednesday

I do not wish us during Lent to begin any sort of argument concerning baptism; the age at which appropriate; the mode; or another ancillary debate apart from the necessity of Trinitarian water baptism, and the universal preamble to the Trinitarian formula, "I baptize you . . ."

> In the first instance such a baptism is not an act of the . . . baptized, but an act of the Church on behalf of the . . . baptized, an act in which the Church, and the people of the Church both individually and corporately, confess that they trust the Gospel so much that they believe that the power of God will save this [baptized one] from death. The Church confesses that the Grace of God which has been sufficient to save the members of the Church is also sufficient for this [newly baptized one]. And the Church and the members of the Church commit themselves to raise and nurture, to love, this person in such a way that he will come to a full maturity and himself confess the faith.[1]

> Too often baptism is profaned in the churches, and, it seems, church people do not realize what a radical action and responsibility is involved in baptizing a child [or adult]. . . . The Grace of God is not vitiated by the stupidity or frivolity of Christians. Even though Christians sometimes invoke the name of God but do not take the matter seriously, God does. The name of God may be invoked vainly, but that Name is never invoked in vain.[2]

---

1. Stringfellow is no doubt referring to infant or children's baptism; the same truth holds for believer's baptism for those with such convictions. Truth is truth regardless of one's chronological age.

2. Stringfellow, *Conscience and Obedience*, 28.

By recognizing God's preeminent part in all that is ontological and everything sacramental, "human beings can be spared the temptations to possess or control, restrict or define, the Word of God; the mystery inherent in truth remains viable and inexhaustible, and the efficiency of the redemptive power of the presence of the Word of God in this world is respected."[3] Freed from that which makes for obsessive/compulsive Christian behavior, we are endowed with the right to be called "children of God," based solely on "believing on his Name" (John 1). I have no need to possess but rather to be possessed; no need to control, but to rather be controlled. I could not, should I be so brash, restrict the Word of God, nor will I ever attempt to begin to define the Word of God. You and I have been "buried with Christ in baptism," according to the Apostle Paul. And all of this is accomplished in the theater of history, in the schematic of time which is the season in which the Word of God is scandalously, in the eyes of the world, active and relentlessly pursuing. We are delivered from ever seeing a purely spiritualized Christianity, it does not exist. If we so go beyond the time-place continuum, we miss God's activity.

> In projecting God beyond history, into the unknown and the unknowable, enthroned, perhaps, before this life or in some afterlife but never in *this* life, out of this world, oblivious of the present existence and grandly indifferent—a ridiculous God, is in fact, no God at all.[4]

For the baptized, God is here in Jesus Christ; it is here and now that the Word of God is "quick and powerful and sharper than any sword with two edges"; and it is in this fallen but redeemed place where the baptized is alive even having been declared dead in Christ's own baptism.

Dead with you, Lord, in baptism, nevertheless I live, yet it is not I but you who live in me. Open my eyes to the deity-in-me post-baptism life and I shall be satisfied. Amen.

3. Stringfellow, *Conscience and Obedience*, 28.
4. Stringfellow, *Private and Public Faith*, 15.

Monday after the First Sunday in Lent

It is impossible to have a Lenten Sunday, even liturgically, because historically Christ is risen from the dead and that is a celebration which takes precedence over any period of individual or corporate discipline or practice. Whatever our encounter be with the Word of God or with the world, "the victor in each specific encounter is Christ."[1] Therefore our celebrations on each Lord's Day in Lent is a Sunday *in* Lent, not a Sunday *of* Lent. This is profoundly important and essential to our Lenten journey. On the one hand we are spending time understanding being "crucified with Christ" (dead in other words), while being "alive in Christ" at the exact and same moment in this present time as in all time, past, present, and future. "The resurrection is impregnated with all that has gone before . . ."[2] Whatever age I am right now includes every age I have been and anticipates all future ages I will be until time is no more as we know it. Therefore, Sundays in Lent represent the same resurrection freedom any Sunday of the year represents: Christ has died; Christ is risen; Christ will come again! There is always the demand in Lent for this pregnant place when discipline gives way to the worship of the awesome God, and the celebration in the deepest sense of the sacrament of the Eucharist. "Christ is crucified in the freedom of the resurrection. He submits to the Cross as a witness to the end of death's power over the world."[3]

Again, in whatever Lenten experience you are being baptized today, the Word of God is the vessel which carries the gospel of grace from God to you. The vestigial remains of death and the evil one are unable to alter your course though they may on occasion

---

1. Stringfellow, *Conscience and Obedience*, 71.
2. Stringfellow, *Conscience and Obedience*, 72.
3. Stringfellow, *Conscience and Obedience*, 15–16.

startle and even unnerve you. "His power over death is effective, not just at the terminal point of a man's life, but throughout his life, during *this* life in *this* world, right now. . . . His resurrection means the possibilities of living in this life, in the very midst of death's works, safe and free from death."[4]

This first Monday of Lent then, is a learning experience, and though forty days have been set aside for special devotion and discipline and confession, Sunday is the applauding of the ultimate outcome of death: that is the death of death and the life everlasting. This is true not only for the individual but for the entire creation. "God was in Christ reconciling the world to himself." "Each specific confrontation between Christ and death and between Christ and one of the principalities as one of the powers of death foreshadows the resurrection, exposes and heralds the overwhelming authority over death which Christ has and holds from the beginning of time to the end of time. And the resurrection encompasses and represents all of these particular historic encounters in a single, consummate, indeed, cosmic disclosure of the triumph of Christ over death."[5] The extraordinary pertinence of the Word of God is that it is universal and victorious. That is why Sunday remains tied to, but aloof from the surrounding Lent. But today, we are back to Lent.

> To put it mildly, then, it is careless and misleading to speak of the action of God in the world in Christ in terms of "making the Gospel relevant" to the secular. The body of Christ lives in the world in the unity between God and the world wrought in Christ, in a sense, the Body of Christ lives in the world as the unity of God and the world in Christ.[6]

There is, therefore, no simplistic aphorism to encompass the immensity of these truths. "It is literally pagan, unbiblical, to recite, 'Jesus is the answer!' The Bible is more definitive, the biblical affirmation is 'Jesus is Lord!'"[7]

4. Stringfellow, *Conscience and Obedience*, 72.
5. Stringfellow, *Conscience and Obedience*, 72.
6. Stringfellow, *Private and Public Faith*, 41.
7. Stringfellow, *Conscience and Obedience*, 13.

MONDAY AFTER THE FIRST SUNDAY IN LENT

Lord, deliver me from the trivial, the easy answer, the Lenten stereotype. Help me to keep a Great Lent while all the while maintaining a Great Grace that maintains eternity's values always in my sacramental view. Amen!

Tuesday after the First Sunday in Lent

Many who read Genesis chapter 1 conclude that God's divine creative work ceased on a "sixth day." Nothing could be further from the truth. Divine creative fiat continued and continues, for God's Word is always coming forth. That places the newness of today very far from the newness of the new. There is, to our detriment, a fundamental misunderstanding here. "The Christian view of God as Creator is not simply, not primarily, that of some Originator of things. Christians know God as One who makes and sustains them and all things in this very moment. Men have life, they have it *this* moment, only because God wishes to give it to men. Even fallen creation, even cursed life, even existence in sin, even men in hate of God are sustained by Him. So to speak of God's sustenance is only to know the saga of Creation is God loving men."[1]

This is precisely why care, effort, endeavor, work, are each one, excluded from Lenten practice. Percy Dearmer wrote in his controversial Lenten hymn, *"Now quit your care,"* and many have found solace in making Lent a positive activity rather than an overtly "caring" effort.

Does this mean we are free from the demands of the life of the gospel? Just the opposite. "*Work out your own salvation for it is God who is at work in you to will and to accomplish his good pleasure.*"

> Biblically, the Holy Spirit names the faithfulness of God to his own creation. Biblically, the Holy Spirit means the militant presence of the Word of God inhering in the life of the whole of creation. Biblically, the Holy Spirit is the Word of God at work both historically and existentially, acting incessantly and pervasively to renew the integrity of life in this world. . . . It was the biblical insight into the

1. Stringfellow, "Life of Worship," 7.

TUESDAY AFTER THE FIRST SUNDAY IN LENT

truth of the Holy Spirit that signaled my own emancipation from religiosity . . . the biblical saga of the Word of God as Agitator, as the Holy Spirit, that assures me that wheresoever human conscience is alive and active, *that* is a sign of the saving vitality of the Word of God in history, here and now.[2]

That said, if indeed we have been made alive in Christ Jesus, there is the guarantee that the Word of God is active vitally in my doing and in God's doing in and through me. This is not an excuse for stagnant Christian living, rather it is the declaration that in the Word of God, active in history, "here and now," I cannot be stagnant. The question is not "What should I be doing?" Rather the question is "What is God doing of which I may become a vital part?"

It is evident to Christian believers that God is Creator. "Christians know that Creation is by Grace. God brings the 'heavens and the earth' and everything that is in them into being because He wishes to do so. 'God has no need of us,' wrote Karl Barth, 'He has no need of the world and heaven and earth; all glory, all beauty, all goodness, and holiness reside in Him. He is sufficient unto Himself. *He is God.*'"[3] As creatures, therefore, we are graced into existence and graced into the kingdom of God. Nothing is left to human ingenuity since all genius for salvation comes from God and is made known in the world through the Word of God.

During these days of Lent, give yourself time to see, hear, and know what God is doing in and with you. There is no list of rules, there is no propositional formula, there is no guide to life. *There is life.*

It is with gratitude for life, for grace, and for your working of my salvation that I approach you, Lord. Receive my thanksgiving in place of my own self-effort; my gratitude in place of my idol-seeking; my resting in place of my previous thoughts of accomplishing the truth of the gospel on my own. Amen!

---

2. Stringfellow, *Politics of Spirituality*, 18.
3. Stringfellow, "Life of Worship," 4.

Wednesday after the First Sunday in Lent

There is nothing more detrimental to one's own spiritual life than to live in such a way that others know you as a poor representative of the gospel of Jesus Christ. Often our self does not divulge to us our own hypocrisy because it is intensely involved in sniffing out the hypocrisy of others. If we do not experience the working of the Holy Spirit in our life, then it is not the fault of the Holy Spirit, but rather a blockage we personally put in God's way. It is called ego, self, flesh, self-will, and the like. We are, because of the fall, people pursued by those things that perpetuate death rather than life. Believers have been given the life of victory, completely accomplished by Jesus Christ, and now what remains are the vestigial remains of sin and evil; and even vestigial remains can cause havoc with one's life *for Jesus Christ.*

> Nothing seems more bewildering to a person outside the Church about those inside the Church than the contrast between how Christians behave in society and what Christians do in the sanctuary.
>
> The contrast is not, I suspect, just taken for granted by outsiders as evidence of the hypocrisy of professed Christians. It is not simply that Christians do not practice what is preached and neglect the authenticate worship by witness. The non-churchman is, I suggest, much more bewildered by the difficulty of discerning either connection or consistency between social action and liturgical event.[1]

Often caught up with the "beauty of holiness" in our worship, we get lost to ethics in our lack of a "beauty of wholeness." Our situation is a long-practiced attempt to do both witness and worship authentically but separately, a thing most impossible. If my

---

1. Stringfellow, *Imposters*, xvi.

witness is not informed and shaped by my liturgical action, it is not gospel witness, and if my liturgical actions are not driven by my need for the Holy Spirit to make me cohesive and consistent, then my worship is vacuous and *moves me nowhere important.*

> The race issue, the fundamental sin that flowed naturally from a nation whose intent was to be economically and socially a city on a hill [a thing left for the New Jerusalem, not New York, the New World, or the New Order]. A new order, granted all the Judeo-Christian seeds it carried and planted, did, nonetheless carry the greatest number of seeds of secularism. Because of this, slavery, and thus racism has been a besetting sin which haunted and continues to haunt us. [And] both captive and captor have the same inheritance.[2]

What we inherit is the need for redemption, or in Stringfellow's word, "absolution." It is a Lenten need which both fathers and sons desperately need; their hearts crave it.

Such a deep-seated hunger is filled solely by Jesus Christ and the cross.

> The Cross is not at all a religious symbol—it is profaned when it becomes that in the minds of men. Nor is the Cross just some reference to an event which took place once upon a time but which has no reality and correspondence to the present day. Rather the Cross means the invincible power of God's love for the world even though all the world betrays, denies, fears or oppresses the gift of this love to the world. The Cross means voluntary love which is unfazed by any hostility or hatred or violence or assault. The Cross means voluntary love which is not threatened by death. The Cross means voluntary love which perseveres no matter what.
>
> The Cross means the gift of love even to one's own enemy—even to the one who would take one's life. . . . In the work of God in our midst in reconciling black men and white men there is no escape from the Cross.[3]

---

2. Stringfellow, *New Theology*, 294.
3. Stringfellow, *New Theology*, 295–96.

God's committing the work of reconciliation to us, 2 Corinthians 5:18–20, means we cannot live reconciled to any other human being without a life-changing sojourn through the cross. The Apostle Paul was unambiguous, "*All this is from God, who reconciled us to himself through Christ and gave us the ministry of reconciliation: that God was reconciling the world to himself in Christ, not counting people's sins against them. And he has committed to us the message of reconciliation. We are therefore Christ's ambassadors, as though God were making his appeal through us. We implore you on Christ's behalf: Be reconciled to God*" (italics Stringfellow's).

During this Lenten journey, walk me mindfully through the cross, making me conscious of my own reconciliation; challenged by your assignment of informing the world of its reconciliation; and being Holy Spirit coherent and consistent in all of this privilege. Amen!

Thursday after the First Sunday in Lent

That Israel worshipped a "golden calf," which many historians tell us may have been less than 12" long and 8" high, is the height of idolatrous paganism. Can you even imagine thousands of people paying homage, giving worthy ritual honor to a figure the size of a toy? It matters not the value or the size really, it was gold. *Gold*, a precious metal even to Hebrews in the desert, was, in their idolatrous minds worthy to be worshipped; God granted freedom, but in their thinking, gold would keep them free, just as "creating wealth" in America in the second decade of the twenty-first century is to be the goal of every American. But remember what happens when God steps into the circumstance.

Moses takes this idol (in the Hebrew language an "idol" is "a nothing"), and pulverizes it into an unrecognizable powder, subsequently making Israel mix it with water and drink it. It therefore passes through the digestive systems of the children of Abraham and is mixed inseparably with their fecal matter. Their idol is now part of human waste and is not even redeemable from the human septic system of life. A gross description, possibly, but a necessary one. The waste pile is the place for human idols (nothings).

> According to Christ's gospel, justification cannot be attained by works of any kind. In contrast, idolatry essentially implies grasping after justification by works of one or another variety—obeying certain rules, pursuing certain values, carrying out certain activities or rituals, and so on. These last become forms of tribute which men offer to what they had enshrined as idols, and so they become dehumanizing, death-dealing.[1]

---

1. Stringfellow, *Imposters*, 7.

Every idol shares with every other idol the inevitable characteristic of being a nothing and playing the part of God. And an idol does not have to be, and usually is not some kind of creative work of art; of course that is possible. Those of us who have been churchmen for any length of time know that "precious" buildings; forms of liturgy or worship; colors of paraments; times of services; and such other ancillary matters to Christianity rise to the level of being idols by many in the church. It is evidence of the reign of death even in the church. It is a sad commentary on Christianity, when idols such as those listed above displace resurrected all-powerful Jesus Christ. The life of Christ bears no parallel to the idols of men, and yet we are given in doing our best to somehow make Christ and the work of our hands exist on par with one another. Many a priest or pastor has moved on from a church because the God who was worshiped in that place is far inferior God found in the gospel of the Word of God.

> All idols are imposters of God. . . . Idolatry is the worship of what man has turned into such an imposter. In other words, idolatry means honoring the idol as that which renders the existence of the idolater morally significant, ultimately worthwhile. The idolater believes that his virtue or worthiness depends upon the consistency, zeal, and appropriateness of the devotion, service, and elevation the records to the idol. . . . Americans who have devoutly served the idols of respectability and status all their lives feel threatened in their very being when their children refuse to offer these idols the same worship. . . . All Christians can speak of justification by faith rather than by works of justification at once personal and cosmic, both immediate and ultimate, nonexclusive but ecumenical. . . . Undeserved, unearned, immeasurable, free and priceless, justification by faith is not essentially concerned with the issue of the faithfulness of men to God, but with the fidelity of God to himself and to mankind, and thus with the faithfulness of men to their humanity.
>
> As Galatians puts it, all services rendered to idols are "works of the flesh," that is, works infected by death, works leading to death not life. . . . The term is being used

here in the manifold connotations of its uses in the Bible: not only physical death but all forms of diminution of human life and development and dignity, and all forms of alienation of men from themselves and from one another and from God. Since idolatry of any kind demeans man, prevents him from becoming fully human, death is that which, under many disguises, idolaters really worship. On the other hand, justification by faith means the integrity of human life as a gift is radically affirmed.

Idolatry thus defies God and dehumanizes men. But it also patronizes and so vitiates what is idolized. For example, when idolatrous patriotism is practiced, the vocation of the nation so idolized is destroyed. When money becomes an idol, the true utility of money is a loss. When the family is idolized the members of the family are enslaved. Every idol, therefore, represents a thing or being existing in a state of profound disorientation.

In other words, idolatry is a manifestation of what, in Christian tradition, is called the Fall. All the tiresome controversies about the historicity of Genesis are quite irrelevant here. In fact they distract our attention from the cogency of the biblical description of men and of institutions and of all creatures as existing in a state of estrangement each from all the others, each suffering from a crisis as to his or its identity.

The Fall thus characterizes *this very day*—or any other day—in the whole of human history—in terms of each man's radical confusion about who he is and the similar bewilderment of other beings and things about what they are. The Fall refers to the ubiquity of alienation between and among each being and all the rest.[2]

Be it national, ecclesial, institutional, personal, familial, and on and on, idolatry is that nothing which we tend to make something, almost everything. When this occurs, the biblical witness evaporates and men become "sounding brass and tinkling cymbals." The world has had enough.

---

2. Stringfellow, *Imposters*, 7–9.

Deliver me from each and every idol of my life. May I, as many in the Bible, "turn from idols to serve the living God"! You have convinced me, O God, I cannot do both simultaneously. Amen!

Friday after the First Sunday in Lent

Many years ago I was "called" by the official board of a large parish to relocate as their senior pastor ("lead pastor" in today's lingo) on the condition that I would take a special kind of training for door-to-door evangelism (to which, then and now, I do not subscribe). I declined the call, on that issue and the fact that God was calling my wife and me into the Episcopal Church. But the idea of a prepackaged evangelism program itself is odious. Evangelization is truth through one's personality which has experienced the salvation of which the gospel speaks. Canned witness is no witness and the Apostle Paul labels such vacuous approaches the witness as "zeal without knowledge." Jesus Christ comingled with people, and thus people followed him; if we will, as the church get to know people, they will want the Jesus Christ our gospel witness exudes.

> It is a work which cannot be done with fanfare lest the uniqueness with which the gospel addresses each man in his own life is vitiated. Nor is there some stereotyped scheme of evangelization. Evangelism is not essentially verbal, even though it seems commonly to be believed that the recitation of certain words constitute efficacious evangelism. Evangelism consists of loving another human being in a way which represents to him the care of God for his particular life. Evangelism rests upon the appeal to another man to remember his own creation—remember who made him and for whom he was made. Evangelism is the event in which a Christian confronts another man in a way which assures the other man that the new life which he observed in the Christian is vouchsafe for him also.[1]

---

1. Stringfellow, *Private and Public Faith*, 54–55.

The gospel, though in provision and in what it produces (the church), is radically individual, for God knows each and every fallen creature and has made unquestionable provision for him individually. "In the gospel men do not sacrifice themselves or their lives or any part of their lives for God. Just the contrary, in the gospel, God sacrifices his life for men."[2]

Lent is not the time to place everyone in the same box (as if anytime is right for that). Lent especially is that time of allowing oneself to be prepared by God for what the resurrection will mean for that which will be encountered in the immediate future. God never calls a man without preparation, and the church has liturgically made a time for that: forty days and forty nights. "Jesus Christ means that God cares extremely, decisively, inclusively, immediately for the ordinary, transient, proud, wonderful, the setting, profane, frivolous, heroic, lusty things of men."[3] Knowing, therefore, that God so intimately cares, knowing that God so intimately knows, and knowing that God so intimately includes each man is gospel freedom as it is intended to be known with integrity.

"Christ means that although in fallen creation vocation is distorted and worship is scandalized, the sovereignty of God is neither disrupted or aborted."[4] Nothing, therefore, thwarts the notorious activity of Jesus Christ. He cannot be stopped in his gospel work.

> The word of God in Christ for the world is the world. The work of God in Christ is God making the world for himself. The original and final, the indigenous and present, the fundamental and radical truth about creation is the Lordship of Jesus Christ. Christ is the Lord: the world and the work of the world in which men engage belong to him. Christ is the Lord: in him is the embodiment of human life which is reconciled within itself and at the same time with both God and all things and all men.[5]

---

2. Stringfellow, *Instead of Death*, 48.
3. Stringfellow, *Private and Public Faith*, 40.
4. Stringfellow, *Conscience and Obedience*, 31.
5. Stringfellow, *Instead of Death*, 45.

FRIDAY AFTER THE FIRST SUNDAY IN LENT

A Great Lent is a time when we are made relevant and witnesses of the gospel and those outside the church take life-changing notice!

Easter Vigil, Lord, as I understand it, is a liturgical provision for those converted to be baptized. May my witness bear the marks of gospel integrity so that one person, at least, may respond to the Word of God, give himself to Christ, and feel the "cleansing flood" of baptismal waters soon. Amen!

Saturday after the First Sunday in Lent

As this is being written in 2019, "religion" has taken a bad rap because it is supposedly dogmatic and defined, and it has been replaced with the concept of "spirituality," which has been determined by some authority to be nebulous, undefined, nonspecific, individual, self-defined, amorphous, without repetition, *ad infinitum*. It seems the Holy Spirit fits our lack of form, rather than the Holy Spirit being the formation power for us. Our danger, especially in Lent is "me-ism," an overt, exclusive, individual, self-defined program to fulfill the self, in place of Lent being a time when we are saved *from self* because our focus is on the church for the world.

> The name of the Holy Spirit is manipulated or defamed throughout the churches . . . it is no wonder that "spirituality" and terms associated with "spirituality" would be recited in disjointed, self-serving, indefinite syntax. Somewhat ironically, there are not only these problems of vagueness and the like with the topic and vocabulary of "spirituality," but also those occasioned by a veritable plethora of references, allusions, or connections. "Spirituality" may indicate stoic attitudes, occult phenomena, the practice of so-called mind control, yoga discipline, escapist fantasies, interior journeys, an appreciation of Eastern religions, multifarious pietistic exercises, superstitious imaginations, intensive journals, dynamic muscle tension, assorted dietary regimens, meditation, jogging cults, monastic rigors, mortification of the flesh, wilderness sojourns, political resistance, contemplation, abstinence, hospitality, a vocation of poverty, nonviolence, silence, the efforts of prayer, obedience, generosity, exhibiting stigmata, entering solitude, or, I suppose, among these and many other things, squatting on top of a pillar.
>
> The clutter associated with what is called spirituality is accentuated, if not fully or adequately explicated,

SATURDAY AFTER THE FIRST SUNDAY IN LENT

by the frequent and familiar commercial exploitation of both the language and the subject of "spirituality" and, to use an appropriate technical term the marketing of "spirituality" to mass constituencies inside the boundaries of American Christendom as well as outside those nominal precincts. The proliferation, in just the past two decades, of sects, therapies, cults, self-discovery movements, ashram's, and similar excursions is literally fantastic and betells a pathetic need which seems to be spawned in the culture itself. At the same time, these developments expose a poignant ridicule of the authentic spirituality vested in the church since the apostolic era and a colossal pastoral default chargeable to the churches. This has rendered "spirituality" vulnerable to commercialization and has caused the yearnings of human beings for spiritual integrity and living—as vague or diffuse as such may be—to be articulated in commercialized versions of the crudest degree.[1]

Such unauthentic witness is not to the Word of God, but rather to the perpetual harassment of death toward each and every one who wishes to live a life of coherence according to the gospel. Spirituality is radically gospel-defined; world-oriented; filled to the brim with the Word of God; and powerfully witnessed to by the Holy Spirit. The opposite is a focus which is radically different in orientation.

> The concentration is usually upon self-realization of some sort disconnected with the rest of created life. . . . There is no biblical spirituality to be found in a vacuum, cut off from the remainder of humanity within the totality of creation. Indeed, biblical spirituality is significantly about the resurrection or renewal of these relationships throughout the realm of created life. To put the same differently, biblical spirituality concerns living in the midst of the era of the fall, wherein all relationships whatsoever have been lost or damaged or diminished or twisted or broken, in such a way which is open to transcendence of the fallenness of each and

---

1. Stringfellow, *Politics of Spirituality*, 19–20.

every relationship and in which these very relationships are recovered or rendered new. . . .

When all is said and done, however, the aspect of the ambivalence of contemporary "spirituality" that provokes me to be most wary, and has chiefly inhibited the use of such language in my own speaking and writing, is the popular interpretation of "spirituality" as a rejection of the most elementary teaching of the New Testament: the Incarnation. Where the syntax of "spirituality" refers to substance and content at all, and is not just some verbose mishmash, it often represents an emulation of the Greek mentality, or similar pagan attitude, in which the body is separated from the spirit, or the flesh from the soul, or the physical from the spiritual, the material from the mental, the tangible from the ethereal, and so on and on. These dichotomies—unbiblical, false, and basically deceptive—quickly lead to collateral distinctions equally offensive to the gospel of Jesus Christ, like those purporting to distinguish between the profane and the sacred, the secular and the sacrosanct, the temporal and the spiritual, the defiled and the pure. What ever quaintness these juxtapositions have poetically, theologically they are hostile to the truth of the incarnation. That is, as far as I am concerned, not a matter of doctrine only. Primarily it is an issue of the denial inherent in such supposed dichotomies of the basic event of the implication of the word of God in the common history of this world in Jesus Christ. It is in that event, it is in what has approximately happened in history in Jesus Christ, that all such separations are abolished.[2]

These truths must shake us, and movingly remind us that the resurrection toward which Lent points, can only be the focus when the incarnation is the foundation. And in the incarnation, God has affirmed that the body is a vital organ of spirituality, like it or not.

---

2. Stringfellow, *Politics of Spirituality*, 21–22.

SATURDAY AFTER THE FIRST SUNDAY IN LENT

Lord, your gospel of Jesus Christ, incarnate in history has convinced me that the Platonic separation of body from soul is a fabrication, a lie, and a message of death. Rather, the body is good and is as much part of my spirituality and the spirituality of the church as is my soul and the souls of all others. Amen.

Monday after the Second Sunday in Lent

Worship is the work of the church. A necessary and subsequent extension of the true and authentic integrity of worship is evangelism. The man who is not a churchman will see gospel worship and his hunger will be enlarged, his thirst will be increased, and he will want what the church possesses. To focus on worship evangelism is to miss each: worship and evangelism. But to place a community of faith so focused on worship that worship becomes evangelism has both biblical mandate and biblical example. The books of Romans and Galatians are nothing if not challenges to the church to make the onlookers, both Jew and Gentile, jealous of their possession by God and the gospel. Lent is a time to jealously, as churchmen, long for deep, true, worship which possesses both liturgy and integrity.

> Worship, though, is not merely some re-enactment of the drama of God and man in Creation. It is the drama itself. It is the same event, not some facsimile, not some representation of the event. When God, therefore, is worshipped in the Church, when God is thus worshipped in history, there is taking place the focal event in history. Moreover it is an event which breaks out of the bounds of history: worship is at once within and beyond history.
>
> This is something of the reality of worship; and it must of course be laid alongside the practice of worship in the churches. And to do so discloses what contemporary practice conceals, often denies, and surely scandalizes the reality of the worship of Almighty God. Yet where God is verily worshipped—when Christians gather as a congregation to baptize a new person or two celebrate the Lord's Supper, or to hear the Word of God—what takes place is the appropriation of things which God has made (i.e. bread, wine, water) to praise Him. What takes

> place is a rendering to God of that which He has given to men. The appropriation in worship is focused upon the sacramental elements more specifically, perhaps, but it extends not only to bread and wine but to the building, the garments, and (most essentially) the people gathered. Everything is given to Him: everything which He first has given to men.[1]

Worship is vitally important!

> A most obstinate misconception associated with the gospel of Jesus Christ is that the gospel is welcome in this world. The conviction endemic among church folk persists that, if problems of misapprehension and misrepresentation are overcome and the gospel can be heard in its own integrity, the gospel will be found attractive by people, become popular and even be a success of some sort. This idea is curious and ironical because it is bluntly contradicted in Scripture, and in the experience of the continuing biblical witness in history from the event of Pentecost unto the present moment. During Jesus' earthly ministry, no one in His family and not a single one of the disciples accepted Him, believed His vocation or loved the gospel He bespoke and embodies. Since the rubrics of success, power, or gain are impertinent to the gospel, the witness of the saints looks foolish where it is most exemplary.[2]

What you have called us (me) to do is to be a person of worship. Make me able to render back to you that with which you have blessed me. May my worship bear the marks of coherent integrity and consistent vitality. Amen!

---

1. Stringfellow, "Life of Worship," 12.
2. Stringfellow, "Living with Defeat," 13–14.

Tuesday after the Second Sunday in Lent

Listening is a rare happening among human beings. You cannot listen to the word another is speaking if you are preoccupied with your appearance or impressing the other, or if you are trying to decide what you are going to say when the other stops talking, or if you are debating about whether the word being spoken is true or relevant or agreeable. Such matters may have their place, but only after listening to the word as the word is being uttered. Listening, in other words, is a primitive act of love, in which a person gives self to another's word, making self-accessible and vulnerable to that word.[1]

Lent is about giving self away; of giving to another the human attention which is due each man. An old Sunday school hymn I recall had the words, by Howard Grose:

> *Give of your best to the Master,*
> *Give of the strength of your youth;*
> *Throw your soul's fresh, glowing ardor*
> *Into the battle for truth.*
> *Jesus has set the example,*
> *Dauntless was He, young and brave;*
> *Give Him your loyal devotion;*
> *Give Him the best that you have.*

"The practice of the Christian life consists of the discernment of (the seeing and hearing), and the reliance upon (the reckless and uncalculating dependence), and the celebration (the ready and spontaneous enjoyment) of the presence of the Word of God in the common life of the world."[2]

1. Stringfellow, *Count It All Joy*, 16.
2. Stringfellow, *Private and Public Faith*, 56.

> Thus the vocation of the baptized person is a simple thing: it is to live from day to day, whatever the day brings, in this extraordinary unity, in this reconciliation with all people and all things, in this knowledge that death has no more power, in this truth of the resurrection. It does not really matter exactly what a Christian does from day to day. What matters is that whatever one does is done in honor of one's own life, given to one by God and restored to one in Christ, and in honor of the life into which all humans and all things are called. The only thing that really matters to live in Christ instead of death.[3]

Living from day-to-day was not always easy for Stringfellow, nor is it for you or for me. In his most deeply personal book, Stringfellow wrote this of his time of pain and seemingly immanent death:

> When I write that my own situation in those months of pain and decision can be described as prayer, I do not only recall that during that time I sometimes read the Psalms and they became my psalms, or that, as I have also mentioned, I occasionally cried "Jesus" and that name was my prayer, but I mean that I also at times would shout "Fuck!" and that was no obscenity, but a most earnest prayerful utterance.
>
> In the final analysis, no matter what the vocabulary of prayer, or where muteness displaces words in prayer, the content—what is communicated by a person in the world before God—in prayer is in each and every circumstance the same and it can be put plainly in one word: Help!
>
> That is the word of Gethsemane's prayer; that is the word of the Lord's Prayer; that is the prayer when Christ repeats the Twenty-second Psalm from the cross.
>
> It is the prayer of Christ interceding for all people, and it is the prayer of a human creature acknowledging God's vocation in affirming the life which God has called into being.[4]

---

3. Stringfellow, *Instead of Death*, 112.
4. Stringfellow, *Second Birthday*, 108–9.

Lord, even when I cannot pray, hear my prayer. Incline your ear in my direction and hear even the loud cries of my silence. May my mute tongue speak volumes of your praise and may you hear it gladly. Amen!

Wednesday after the Second Sunday in Lent

The absolute power of the name of Jesus Christ as manifest in the gospel, the revelation of God in the Word of God, and the present notorious action of God in the world coalesce to make the believer aware that he is *not alone*. Not even in the deepening darkness of Lent as Passion Week approaches can the Light "which enlightens everyone who comes into the world" (John 1:9) be extinguished no matter how dim it may appear. "The venerable argument as to whether or not in the tactics of evangelism one finally has to name the Name is answered in the fact that Jesus Christ is the historic, unique, and universal verification of God's presence in this history in this world."[1]

There is no place for or need of guesswork, or vacuous hoping as to the God to whom we travel during Lenten journeys or any other journey we may take in the integrity of our spirituality.

> This Gospel of Jesus Christ ends all speculations; demolishes all merely religious ceremonies and sacrifices appeasing unknown gods; destroys every exclusiveness which religion attaches to itself in God's name; attests that the presence of God is not remote, distant, and probably out-of-reach, but here, now, and with us in this world, already. This Gospel means that the very life of God is evident in this world, in this life, because Jesus Christ once participated in the common life of men in this history of our world.[2]

As each of us addresses our own sin in the Lenten journey, we are encouraged and have hope within our grasp that the reality

---

1. Stringfellow, *Instead of Death*, 52.
2. Stringfellow, *Private and Public Faith*, 15.

of sin in the entire created order is only overcome by the act of Jesus Christ—that act of ultimate reconciliation of the universe with God. Apart from this there is indeed a weight which man cannot bear.

> The Biblical description of sin is not so much the designation of certain kinds of conduct as sin—in sex, or in any other realm of human life—as it is the usurpation by men of the prerogative of God in judging all human decisions and actions. Every specific act—every thought, word, and deed—of every person, and, as well, of every institution and nation, is subject to *that* judgment, and *that* judgment in no wise mitigated, altered, or influenced by the opinions of men, or any man, or society as to that which is in truth good or evil. Or, to put it a bit differently, the Christian knows and confesses that in all things—in every act and decision—men are sinners and that in no way, by any ingenuity, piety, sanction, or social conformity, may a man escape from the full burden of the power of sin over his whole existence.[3]

Lent invites us to relinquish our lives—to "give them away" if you will. "It is in giving that we are receive," intoned St. Francis.

> Wherever we turn we shall discover that God is already there. Therefore, wherever it be, fear not, be thankful, rejoice, and boast in God.
>
> The power to discern God's presence in common life is imparted when one becomes a Christian, an event in which the power of the Word of God in one's personal history is manifest over and over against the power of death. Then and thereafter the Christian lives to comfort other men, whatever their afflictions, with the news of God's care for the world. Then and thereafter the threat of his historic death holds no fear for the Christian, for there is nothing which he will on that day experience which he has not already foretasted in the event of his becoming a Christian, in the event of his surrender to the power of death and of his being saved from the power by the presence of God. Then and thereafter he is free from

---

3. Stringfellow, *Instead of Death*, 36.

WEDNESDAY AFTER THE SECOND SUNDAY IN LENT

the most elementary and universal bondage of men: the struggle to manifest and preserve, whatever the cost, his own existence against that of all other men. Then and thereafter he is free to give his present life away, since his life is secure in the life of God.[4]

One writer reminded us to "die before you die, you'll have no chance thereafter." The Apostle Paul directs us to "reckon yourself dead indeed. . . ." It's odd, Lord, I don't "feel" dead because I go on living. Instruct me in the logic of "reckoning," so that Jesus Christ is seen by others, not me, myself. Amen!

---

4. Stringfellow, *Private and Public Faith*, 66.

Thursday after the Second Sunday in Lent

Lent must remind us, and remind us well, that it is the church to which we have been joined by becoming a Christian and not some brick-and-mortar institutional amalgamation to which we must give proper loyalty to keep it going no matter the cost. The church is both visible and invisible, universal and local, but that does not mean a local manifestation may not morph or close or yoke or be made a mission or preaching station or any one of an infinite number of outbreaking works of God. The surreptitious nature of the temptation to perpetuate an institution is as real as any other temptation and possibly more profoundly dangerous.

> First of all, the Christian (the Church) must simply be in the world in and caring eloquently and honestly for the life of the ordinary world—or the life of any man—just as it is.[1]

> The institutional principalities also make claims upon men for idolatrous commitment in that the principle which governs any institution. . . . Everything else must finally be sacrificed to the cause of preserving the institution, and it is demanded of everyone who lives within its sphere of influence—officers, executives, employees, members, customers, and students—that they commit themselves to the service of that end, the survival of the institution.[2]

> Many other principalities and variations thereof which are familiar in the world today could be identified and named. Money is such a power. Such folk heroes of the country as George Washington, Jefferson Davis, and Abraham Lincoln are principalities. Sex, fashion, and

---

1. Stringfellow, *Conscience and Obedience*, 42.
2. Stringfellow, *Conscience and Obedience*, 55–56.

sports are all among the angelic powers. The image of motherhood or that which Philip Wylie calls "momism" is one of the powers. In England, the institution of the Crown is a principality. Patriotism is such a power. Religion, as distinguished from the Christian faith, is a principality. Men are encompassed in their ordinary daily lives by a great constellation of principalities.[3]

Currently, America is seeing identity politics on the rise—any identity which is more descriptive than "human being," is a principality. Congress is a principality as is political party. New congressmen are a principality—and let's hasten to say the "old guard"—is a principality. CNN is a principality. Fox News is a principality, and so are the personalities on any of these networks.

We only escape identifying with one or more principalities by identifying with *the Principality, the Power* Jesus Christ as revealed in the Word of God and as the illimitable power of the gospel. "*Christian human being*" might just do.

"To speak or act confessionally, coherently, biblically, in problems of conscience in nation or church—for that matter, to deal in biblical terms with ethics at all—is, thus, an endeavor a radical variance from the way in which such issues are posted in the world."[4]

Lord, I need you to deliver me and then my thinking from identifying anything—anything as a greater loyalty than Jesus Christ. It is so difficult to not think with the crowd. Help me to protest the "principality and power" groupthink. May I, because it would please you, think with the mind of Jesus Christ. Amen!

---

3. Stringfellow, *Conscience and Obedience*, 59–60.
4. Stringfellow, *Conscience and Obedience*, 25.

Friday after the Second Sunday in Lent

Idolatry is so powerful a temptation and so grave a sin, that during Lent we must address it as thoroughly as our souls and minds demand. Stringfellow addresses it in practically every book, and of course wrote one book with idolatry as the major theme: *Imposters of God: Inquiries into Favorite Idols*. "There is no issue or event anywhere or anytime which is not addresses by the Gospel which is not the responsibility of the body of Christ. The matters which occupy and preoccupy the daily attentions of secular existence are the issues which claim the attention of the Christian faith. . . . The people and the things with which an ordinary Christian comes into contact from day to day are the primary and most profound issues of his faith and practice."[1] However, each good thing has a tendency to become a god (small "g") thing. As god things they attempt to reign over us, claim exclusive loyalties, and insult the gospel of Jesus Christ.

> Each principality claims a man's loyalty, service, and worship; each makes essentially the same demands that a man regard it as his god; as the one in the idolatry of which a man's life will gain moral significance. Each makes the same claim, but a man is beset by the several claims of the principalities of class, race, nation, profession, and family; all made more or less at the same time and each insistent upon taking precedence over everything else. . . . But this bewildering and intensely complex array of principalities exists in the world not only in conflict with the lives of men.[2]

National exceptionalism is an idol; "the mere practice of religion has become the substitute for the Gospel, that is, for

1. Stringfellow, *Conscience and Obedience*, 16.
2. Stringfellow, *Conscience and Obedience*, 60.

FRIDAY AFTER THE SECOND SUNDAY IN LENT

the knowledge of God which God Himself gives to men in Jesus Christ. Perhaps American Protestantism just does not want the Gospel anyway."[3]

> The survival of the nation as such becomes the idol, the chief object of loyalty, service, and idolatry. Or, to put it a bit differently, the historic ideological realities in American history, those of capitalism and democracy, are now displaced by elementary nationalism. But in any case the pre-eminent fact in terms of which, it is claimed, men will find their own justification is in service to the nation, in the offering of all other things for the sake of national survival. Or, in the inaugural words of President Kennedy, "Ask not what your country can do for you; ask what you can do for your country."[4]

Do we realize this is a bastardization, an adulterating of the God-designed way things are to be? The Bible speaks with an integrity and coherence quite differently than these idolatrous voices.

> But when, now and then, I turn to and listen to the Bible, or when, now and then, I hear the Word of God exposed in preaching, or when, now and then, I see the Gospel represented in the Holy Communion and I thereupon become a participant in and witness of the real life which is given to the world, or when, now and then, I meet some Christian, or when, now and then, I discern the presence of God's Word in the ordinary affairs of everyday existence in the world—on these occasions, in these circumstances, I am reminded, if sometimes ruefully, that the Gospel is no mere religion in *any* essential respect.[5]

Lord God, you are so much more immense than my idols; help me to turn from their puniness to your enormity that my soul will also be made large. Help me to know that to know you is to be larger on the inside than on the outside; and that idols reverse that reality to my death. Amen!

3. Stringfellow, *Private and Public Faith*, 26.
4. Stringfellow, *Conscience and Obedience*, 58.
5. Stringfellow, *Private and Public Faith*, 14.

Saturday after the Second Sunday in Lent

The man who claims Christ as his loyalty must know that it is in action, not in mere words, that a witness to the gospel is proclaimed. Everyone is readily convinced that mere preaching is completely inadequate to the Christian witness if it is not coherently and with integrity conjoined with practice. "Practice what you preach" is hardly a new aphorism. "A Christian is distinguished by his radical esteem for the Incarnation—to use the traditional jargon—by his reverence for the life of God in the whole of Creation, even and, in a sense, especially Creation in the travail of sin."[1] "This is because there are no disincarnate issues."[2] There is nothing in the Christian believer's life which exists free from the incarnate history and reality of the gospel record—a record which powerfully proclaims the deliverance from the fall, the reality of the reign of death.

> The Christian in secular society is always in the position of a radical—not in the conventional political sense of that word, but in the sense that nothing which is achieved in secular life can ever satisfy the insight which the Christian is given as to what the true consummation of life in society is. The Christian always complains of the STATUS QUO, whatever that happens to be; he always seeks more than that which satisfies even the best ideals of other men. Or, to put it differently, the Christian knows that no change, reform, or accomplishment of secular society can modify, threaten, or diminish the active reign of death in the world. Only Christ can do that, and now his reign is acknowledged and enjoyed in the society which bears his name and has the task of

---

1. Stringfellow, *Private and Public Faith*, 43.
2. Stringfellow, *Conscience and Obedience*, 25.

proclamation in all the world for the sake of that part of the world still consigned to the power of death.[3]

Those not churched have issue with the gospel witness, and often with the one giving a witness of integrity. This, of course, does not mean that we mitigate the demands and directives of the gospel, but rather that we remain true to our confession. A coherent witness is a gospel witness. "What really scandalizes non-Christians is the confession on the part of Christians that God lives and *works:* that is the awful scandal of the gospel. To confess God in this way is not an affection for 'moral and spiritual values' nor is it a persuasion to some splendid idea of God, or just a religious vocabulary dressing up ordinary social morality, or some sublime speculative truth, but it is confession of God's real presence—His life, power, vitality, action, and working in and for this world."[4]

We cannot fall into the trap of thinking we convert others. We must see evangelism and conversion are two sides of the same coin; two actions in the salvation scheme; two actions, one ours and one God's. "Evangelism is a work of the Church: conversion is a work of God. Evangelism calls men to remember and recognize the presence and activity of God in their own particular lives. Conversion is the event of that recall and recognition."[5]

The whole world "turns upside down" according to G. K. Chesterton; feet once dancing groundless in the air become firmly planted on the ground and the mind once planted in the soil is right-side-up, brought closest to God.

"Existentially and empirically, the reconciliation of the world with God in Jesus Christ establishes a man in unity with both God and the whole world. The singular life of the Christian is a sacrament—a recall, a representation, and enactment, a communication—of that given actual unity, whether in the gathering of the

---

3. Stringfellow, *Conscience and Obedience*, 44.
4. Stringfellow, *Instead of Death*, 44.
5. Stringfellow, *Instead of Death*, 53.

worshipping congregation now and then or whether in the scattering of the members within the daily affairs of the world."[6]

Lord, help me to eschew those things I am told about withdrawing from the "daily affairs of the world." Use your Holy Spirit to make my mind and my actions notoriously active—a sign that life indeed is a sacrament—is sacramental. Amen!

---

6. Stringfellow, *Private and Public Faith*, 40.

Monday after the Third Sunday in Lent

Children can be Christian, too. Sounds so trite does it not? But the church has often made children or youth out to be "the church of the future." I am always offended at that remark: I was offended at fifteen and I continue to be offended at sixty-seven. I am still the church of the future, here on earth for some more years, I would hope, and then with the church triumphant in paradise upon physical death; body and soul separated until the eschaton and the final recapitulation of all things in Jesus Christ. But youth are the church today and I can, if necessary give a strong apologetic for this position I take (and which Stringfellow took, as well).

Your children may be grown and gone; you may have young people or toddlers around your home; you may be without children, but whatever the circumstance, you and I are members of the church, the gospel-formed community where children and youth are *now*, *not later* as important as those septuagenarians who are members of the church. Therefore this reading is for all of us—without excuse.

"The Call of this conference"[1] declares that

> much that we have counted on in the past seems inadequate.... Our faith in the Church and in religious curricula, our dependence on parental standards and school ideals, and our reliance on conventional society and the dictates of the human heart have not been able to combat the instability, moral confusion, and aimlessness so widespread among young people.... My response to that assertion is that, if true, it proves the instability, moral confusion, and aimlessness of faith in the Church, and in religious curricula, dependence on parental standards

---

1. Stringfellow, "Crisis Accepted," 35.

and school ideals, and reliance upon conventions of society and the dictates of the human heart.

The crisis which young people in private and—let them not be overlooked—in public education face today is *not* specifically their own moral decadence or absence of purpose or bewilderment. The crisis of youth, and, for that matter, the crisis of their elders, today concerns the unreliability, corruption, and obsolescence of many of the inherited institutions, policies, laws, standards, and presuppositions of this society.

The sins of the fathers may be visited upon the sons, but that does not thereby absolve the fathers.

As a Christian I remember that men are always in crisis. Crisis is the very theme portrayed in the third chapter of the Book of Genesis. It is a crisis to be sent forth from the womb. Crisis is not some peculiar affliction of mid-twentieth-century America or of the adolescent population—least of all of its tiny minority of prep school students. So let none be astonished or unduly distressed by crisis nowadays. Of course there is crisis: crisis is the normative human situation, empirically, historically, and biblically. Crisis, far from being some novel occasional, or recent occurrence is, in truth, a synonym for the Fall. . . . And let us remember that "the Fall" placed all men in a box—each the same, fallen, out of relationship, idolaters, and on and on. And for you, for me, there is no redemption in the box—not for anyone. It is the cohesive content of the Gospel, the substance of the Word of God alone which will keep each man [and young person] in the crisis of knowing the God who is active in history.[2]

If the young do not discern what the elders are talking about when they prattle about "the dictates of the human heart," they expose the truth that their elders have not a clue to what they are talking about either when they invoke such literally meaningful clichés, and thereby the young do adults a profound service by recalling their parents and teachers from aimlessness and cant. If the youth balk at being poured into a mold, resist being

2. Stringfellow, "Crisis Accepted," 40–41.

coerced into conformity, refuse to surrender meekly to the status quo without, at least, a struggle let everyone else rejoice that the young still possess some stamina, some guts, and some hope. And if adolescents have no faith in the Church and in religious curricula surely the whole communion of saints will cheer out loud, for maybe, if freed from churchiness and superstition and Sunday-school fairy tales, they will instead embrace the Gospel of Jesus Christ.[3]

It is with a great desire for awareness that I pray today for the integrity of faith and life which will make a gospel appeal to the young as well as the old in my circle of influence. Deliver me, for it is my will to be delivered from ecclesiastical baggage and to be faithful to the gospel of Jesus Christ. Amen!

---

3. Stringfellow, "Crisis Accepted," 41–42.

Tuesday after the Third Sunday in Lent

Remember, Stringfellow graduated Harvard Law School and moved to East Harlem, New York City, to work with the poor and underprivileged. References in today's reading come autobiographically out of that reality:

> There were other fronts which required attention besides the politics of the city and the practice of law in Harlem. I had come initially to Harlem as a member of the group ministry of the East Harlem Protestant Parish, out of concern for the mission of the Church to the poor and to those socially discriminated against in the city.
>
> When I first moved to the neighborhood the parish was suffering from a terrific confusion as to the nature of the Church and the meaning and manner of the Church's task in a place such as Harlem. At the heart of these issues were some of the same matters which so divide the several churches outside of Harlem. They provoked deep divisions within the parish, particularly among members of the group ministry, who, apart from myself and one other man, were clergymen.
>
> Through its first years in the neighborhood the parish had become deeply conformed to the world. Conformity to the world is a temptation which assails the Church no less in the slums than in the suburbs. Conformity to the world exists whenever and wherever the Church regards its message and mission to be primarily determined by, or essentially dominated by, the ethos of secular life and the society which surrounds the Church.... The young ministers ... were much tempted to such conformity. They had seen the Protestant churches abandon the inner city, both physically and psychologically, and were aroused by this attachment and conformity of Protestantism to middle-class American society. They would bring the

ministry of Protestantism back to the inner city and work there among the poor and the dispossessed. In doing so they were confronted with how the ministry would be exercised in the midst of the long-festering, complex, and, to them—since they were white middle—and upper-class people—unfamiliar social problems that characterize urban slum society. To these problems they brought two things—a hostility toward the conventional churches outside the slums, which caused them to think they had little or nothing to learn from the Church outside East Harlem, and a sincere passion for social change and revolution, even. These two emotions joined to underscore the view that before the Gospel could be preached and received by the people of the slums, the way for the Word had to be prepared by improving the education of the people, renovating their housing, finding jobs for them, clearing the streets of garbage and debris, challenging the political status quo, alleviating the narcotics problem, and by social action of all sorts. When some of these issues had been resolved, when the lives of the people were less burdened with poverty, discrimination, illiteracy, and ignorance, then the time would come to preach the Gospel and then the people, no longer preoccupied with their afflictions, would be able to hear and embrace the Gospel. One of the earlier parish documents declares that the parish "is a group of ministry of twelve men and women working at the neighborhood level to help people face and work on their problems." Ironically, in spite of their rejection of middle-class Protestantism, the group ministry initially seems to have seen its task as making the East Harlem neighborhood more nearly middle-class! Such a prejudgment is marred by the same sort of confusion that beset many missionaries who, in the early days of American foreign missions, went to Africa, Latin America, and the Far East, and who thought that before the people indigenous to those places could understand and receive the Word of God in Christ, they had to be Westernized. . . .

In any event, the preaching and service of the Gospel do not depend upon any special social change, ideationally or in any other way. The Gospel does not even depend upon the American way of life, either in its integrity or its breach.[1]

Have any of us who have read this said, "Ouch!?" Stringfellow is spot on concerning the freedom of the gospel—its absolute refusal to be subject to anything or anyone—its supreme power over all the acolytes of death, whatever their identity.

I have been guilty, Lord, of many times trying to ease the outward needs while ignoring or postponing the inner need of people for the gospel. Instill in me the authenticity of being a gospel-bearer first—it seems other important matters will occupy their important place once the Word of God becomes for me and to me, primary. Amen!

---

1. Stringfellow, *My People Is the Enemy*, 85–87.

Wednesday after the Third Sunday in Lent

The traditions and ethics of the inherited, white denominations—as their adherents sense privately, and everyone else acknowledges openly—are moribund, nostalgic for a legendary past, extravagantly irrelevant to virtually anything to which one might attempt to relate them. White Christendom's institutions are truly secular, that is, utterly preoccupied with their own survival, and hence dissipated in anxiety. Their human constituency is being visibly depleted by dropouts, deaths, and other departures. The people of these churches have been stunned by the renunciation voiced by their own offspring, bewildered by the long overdue rejection of their paternalism by the blacks, and so traumatized by their guilt that their conscience has been both perverted and paralyzed. They have feted a doctrine of achievement in work and in charity that is bereft of biblical authority and that now turns out not even to have the illusion of efficacy. After seeking a justification that proved futile, they grow frantic and afraid, increasingly tempted to an anger that only a false righteousness can spawn.

The condition of white Christendom is pathological; it is, I suggest, the state designated in the Bible as "hardness of heart."

The reason for this bitter ailment is that the white churches in America have long doubted the very existence, much less the vitality, of the Holy Spirit. In these denominations, on the whole, it has never been seriously granted that God has freedom and discretion in being present and active in this world; it has never been conceded that God is not dependent upon human beings and, specifically, upon the white, American bourgeois. It has been presumed instead that God needs these churches, that God's integrity requires their effort, that God's existence in history is verified by their prosperity, popularity, and power. Today, with the legitimacy of their wealth under challenge, their reputation the butt of ridicule, and their power ineffectual, it becomes clear that their god is indeed dead and, even more threatening, that their god is not and never was God.[1]

Stringfellow wrote this in 1969. When I discovered this writing was in summer of 2019. I, as a white American Christian male of sixty-seven years, was at once convicted. I am assured by church history and practice that Lent is a time for conviction, for the Holy Spirit to "needle our consciences." "It is time for judgment to begin in the house of God," echoes in the Word of God.

> It is the ubiquity of God's judgment—extending to every time and place—and the universality of God's judgment—reaching to every man and principality or power—and the secrecy of God's judgment—which embraces all creation—taken together with such knowledge as the of the character of God's judgment—namely that His judgment is a facet of His Grace—that authorizes the emphasis of Saint Paul on the extraordinary freedom of the Christian, in making decisions, from anxiety about how those decisions are judged by God.[2]

Understanding that God's judgment is a facet of his grace is an unsettling comfort for the Christian. Professor David Yeago captures today's truth, "God's wrath is the militant refusal of the love of God to settle for less than it intends for his beloved."

Lord, thank you for your judgment which marries itself to your love. My desire is to understand how you can judge and love from the same gospel place. I do not doubt—and I believe even though I do not completely comprehend. "Help thou my unbelief." Amen!

---

1. Prodigal Kiwi(s) blog, "William Stringfellow: White Christendom in America Survives Pathetically," October 2, 2017, https://prodigal.typepad.com/prodigal_kiwi/william_stringfellow/.

2. Stringfellow, *Second Birthday*, 91.

Thursday after the Third Sunday in Lent

As I have stressed, being holy, becoming and being a saint does not mean being perfect but being whole; it does not mean being exceptionally religious, or being religious at all, it means being liberated from religiosity and religious pietism of any sort; it does not mean being morally better, it means being exemplary; it does not mean being godly, it means being truly human; it does not mean being otherworldly, but it means being deeply implicated in the practical existence of this world without succumbing to this world or any aspect of this world, no matter how beguiling. Being holy means a radical self-knowledge; a sense of who one is; a consciousness of one's identity so thorough that it is no longer confused with the identity of others, of persons or of any creatures or of God or of any idols.

For human beings, relief and remedy from such profound confusion concerning a person's own identity and the identity and character of the Word of God becomes the indispensable and authenticating ingredient of being holy, and it is the most crucial aspect of becoming mature—or of being fulfilled—as a human in this world, in fallen creation. This is, at the same time, the manner through which humans can live humanly, in sanity and with conscience, in the fallen world as it is. And these twin faculties, sanity and conscience—rather than some sentimental or pietistic or self-serving notion of moral perfection—constitute the usual marks of sanctification. That which distinguishes the saint is not eccentricity but sanity, not perfection, but conscience.[1]

---

1. Stringfellow, *Politics of Spirituality*, 32–33.

In other words, our sanctification is God through authentic personality—the Word of God defining viscerally who the holy man really is. There is no fanfare for the holy—only faithfulness.

One day on the Amtrak train from upstate New York to my place of employment in New York City, I was queued with others to exit at Penn Station when the train stopped. I was wearing clericals and the man in front of me turned, looked at my black shirt and collar, and simply said, "Oh, a holy man." That was all. And my immediate thought was, "Oh that it were that simple—and oh how misguided he was—clothes nor career make for holiness." Stringfellow caught this truth early in life.

> My own realization of ambiguity and my emphatic repudiation of moral simplistics came, as might have been anticipated, in the making of an actual decision: I decided, at fourteen, not to become a priest. . . . It was made fiercely—more than likely because I was only in my early teens at the time. . . . *I would be damned if I would be a priest.* That was what I decided. I would not be a priest and, moreover, I would spend my life refuting any, who suppose, that to be serious about the Christian faith required ordination. I would be a Christian in spite of the priesthood, in spite of all the priests, in spite of the priest who had, as I saw it at the time, importuned me.
>
> Vocation pertains to the whole of life, including work, of course, if and where there is work, but embracing every other use of time, every other engagement of body or mind, every other circumstance in life.[2]

So the collar doesn't designate or define holiness; identity derived from the Word of God is the secret.

God, reveal, as needed, the counter intuitive truth of what being holy is actually about. Deliver me from the simple definitions and deliver me into the understanding of the depths of meaningful spirituality free from the religiosity churchly society has erected all around. Amen!

---

2. Stringfellow, *Second Birthday*, 80, 82, 94.

Friday after the Third Sunday in Lent

In American culture, and, I suspect, everywhere else, the name of God is terribly maligned. For one thing, the name *God* is seldom any longer used as a name, and that in itself is a literal curse addressed to God. To take a very obvious and familiar example, when Ronald Reagan, in his pronouncement on the school prayer issue and otherwise says, "God," it is difficult to fathom what he may be fantasizing, though it would appear, at most, that he is imagining some idea of god. Sometimes he himself clarifies that my inserting a prefix and speaking of "his god" or "our god" or, also, "their god" while mentioning, as Raegan perceives the situation, and alien or enemy people.[1]

There is a need to contemporize this since it was written in 1984 and personnel have changed—the secularizing of "God" has not. Do we secularize the name and person of "God?"

Yet, *no* idea of god is God; no image of god is God; no conception of god, however appealing or, for that matter however true, coincides with the living God—which the biblical witness bespeaks—present, manifest; militant in common history, discernible in the course of events through the patience and insight of ordinary human beings. The living God, whose style and character the Bible reports, is subject now, as in the biblical era, to the witness of human beings, to their testimony describing what they have beheld of the intent, involvement, self-disclosure, effort, and concern of the Word of God in this world. And so, with as much standing or authority as our predecessors in the faith had long ago, biblical people in this day attest to God as he is revealed in this history, as the *Word of God,*

---

1. Stringfellow, *Politics of Spirituality*, 33. Replace "Ronald Reagan" with any president's name; it matters not which president you choose.

the very same One to whom the biblical witness refers and in which the biblical witness so much rejoices.

When, therefore, I use this name for God, it is deliberately intended to invoke the scriptural saga of the Word of God active in common history from the first initiative of creation. Simultaneously I refer (as, so the say, both Isaiah and John *insist*), the selfsame Word of God incarnate in Jesus Christ. At the same time, I mean to recall the Word of God permeating the whole of creation and ready to be discerned in all things whatsoever in the fallenness of this world; and, again, the Word of God as the Holy Spirit, a work contemporaneously, incessantly agitating change in this world (as the event of Pentecost and the Acts of the Apostles each verify).[2]

Accommodation to the secular world is precisely what the Word of God has power to keep from happening. The Holy Spirit is active at this very moment of time; no waiting; no begging; no groveling; no asking sometimes—but present and active if we will open the mind to his activity. Stringfellow traces this secularization back to Constantine and his marrying the church off to the polis. "It is the Constantinian Arrangement which has fostered, in numerous versions and derivations, through the centuries, such a religioning of the Gospel that its biblical integrity is corrupted and such an acculturation of the Church that it becomes practically indistinguishable from the worldly principalities so that both Gospel and Church become adjuncts or conveyances of civil religion and of a mock-sanctified status of political authority."[3]

Let the gentle flow of church into social work and the confusion of doing cultural things as church work be two temptations from which you protect me. Help me the earliest pull toward either of these to feel and to resist with biblical wholeness and holiness. Amen!

---

2. Stringfellow, *Politics of Spirituality*, 34.
3. Stringfellow, *Conscience and Obedience*, 49.

Saturday after the Third Sunday in Lent

> And he walks with me and he talks with me;
> And he tells me I am his own.
> And the joy we share as we tarry there:
> None other, has ever, known.
>
> —C. Austin Miles (19th Century)

> When he was on the Cross, I was on his mind.
> —Bill & Gloria Gaither (hymn title)

Two sets of musical words, over one hundred years apart in having been written, but each stressing that "I" am the reason for Christ's incarnation, crucifixion, and resurrection.

And though that is true in a sense, the incarnation, crucifixion, and resurrection are for *all humankind; really the recapitulation of the created order to God's purposeful intent.* The lyrics lead us to religion—so rejected by my generation—the sexagenarians—religion rejected for what, in its place people mistakenly called, "spirituality." Actually, it became what these lyrics hint at, a radical "me-ism." So profoundly did this take over in Western culture, that "me-ism" now defines not only spirituality, but politics and the entire social order. We have become a culture of single individuals who tolerate, to one degree or another, other people. Stringfellow addresses the same.

"Religion beguiled me, but I was also beginning to comprehend that the Gospel was, somehow not about religion, but reached beyond religion."[1]

> The radical emphasis for so many generations in American Protestantism upon the individual and upon

---

1. Stringfellow, *Second Birthday*, 81.

> individualistic action as the main theme and form of Christian witness has contributed to the loss among church people of their identification and community with all baptized persons. . . . And, as often as not, the fact which unites such a sect or parish is not baptism into the Body of Christ and the company of the whole Church throughout the ages, but a particular credo pertaining to moral behavior, dress, class, race, social custom, or sometimes just the personality of a preacher or legends associated with the founder of the group. Churchly bodies such as these hardly commend themselves to the nations as models of the new society in Christ.[2]

"Where the Church represents the world reconciled to God and within itself, where the Church lives as Christ's Body, where the Church heralds the judgment of the world by Christ, the Church suffers the same hostility of the world that Christ Himself bore."[3] This doesn't ring true with a walk in a cool garden with gnostic-like secret messages whispered by an innocuous Holy Spirit does it? We, not I, alone, represent the reconciliation completed by Jesus Christ and announced in the Gospel to the needy world.

> For those who become members of the Body of Christ in the world, dominion is restored. The Christian is a man who, by the work of Christ, has had his own life restored to him, is free from the threat of death in all things, and who lives now in reconciliation with other men and with the rest of creation.[4]

Living in reconciliation with others, will lead us to "I" in our personal confession and devotion, and "we" in all the work of Christ in the work of reconciliation given to us in our own new relationship with the Word of God.

---

2. Stringfellow, *Conscience and Obedience*, 104.
3. Stringfellow, *Instead of Death*, 46.
4. Stringfellow, *Instead of Death*, 47.

SATURDAY AFTER THE THIRD SUNDAY IN LENT

Jesus, I want to hear your voice, of course, but I want to hear your voice to the church, to the body of Christ so I may better be in a place to make redemptive change which reaches beyond mere religion into the places where principalities and powers need to be overthrown. Use me as a part of the "we" who compose the church. Amen!

Monday after the Fourth Sunday in Lent

Instead of being somehow transported "out of this world," rather than indulging abstinence, evasion or escapism, rather than fabricating some isolation or separation or privation, the irony of being holy is that one is plunged more fully into the practical existence of this world, as it is, than in any other way.

The irony of being holy contains, of course, no surprising news; it is no more than a manner of stating the New Testament enjoinder for those who follow Jesus to be in the world but not of the world.

An implication of the call to live in the word as it is with utter vulnerability—even, indeed unto the risk of death—and an implication of the rejection of any notion of spirituality as some kind of super piety, yields a second or parallel irony. Commercialized or religiose or other ersatz forms of spirituality typically conformity to the world and avail no freedom from conformity to the regime of the world, even though they boast their own spiritual jargon or assert transcendental goals. Such conformity, though it may assume attractive guises, as was the case for Jesus when he was confronted with the power of death in the wilderness, *always* means conformity to death. And, as the experience of Jesus verifies, the issue in such temptation is not one of merely compromising principle; the issue is becoming an idolator of the power of death.[1]

An immediate response might be, how can I do this—there is no way, through mere wishing, that I can muster the free will and the subsequent willpower to stay with this reality of holiness. It seems every effort is without permanent fruit-bearing; it is a struggle and not a freedom. Stringfellow does not leave us in the precarious place but flays open the splendor of how we are made holy:

1. Stringfellow, *Politics of Spirituality*, 35–36.

The restoration of the original identity of a person—in all its particularities and all its relationships, in the totality of its political significance—the renewal of a person's wholeness, which is the initiation into holiness, is utterly the effort of the Word of God. There is no interpretation which is attributable to a person's ambition, attainment, discipline, works, or merit. The renewal of creation, including the restoration of integrity to persons, is a matter of the Grace of the Word of God. It is a generous gift indeed, as I have already mentioned, encompassing the restoring of relationships within a person and between that person and all other persons, all principalities and powers, nature and the residuum of creation. The gift is also precocious because it is offered *now*, in the midst of the fall, in a way that disrupts, challenges, and resists the apparent sovereignty of the power of death in the world. That means, in turn, that this is an experience which shatters time and liberates people from the confinement of time by at once recalling all that has gone before and anticipating all that is to come.[2]

Vain and fruitless is the struggle, self to sanctify;
God alone can cleanse and keep you,
Wherefore, wherefore should you try?
Oh! the needless cares and conflicts
You had never known,
If you'd learned the simple lesson:
Let yourself, yourself, alone.

—Albert B. Simpson (19th century)

I give up, God . . . I acknowledge I cannot drum up the simple day-to-day coherence of being holy. I accept that being holy is a gift, and I accept that gift. I am grateful for your grace and know it is always giving as I am given to always receiving. Amen!

---

2. Stringfellow, *Politics of Spirituality*, 34–35.

Tuesday after the Fourth Sunday in Lent

The surreptitious nature of that which parades as spirituality, especially in American culture, is the only way such bogus holiness ideas can enter the consciousness. It is an attempt of death to reclaim lost territory.

Without making pretentious judgments, it is possible to discern where conformity . . . is involved and to identify some marks that betell this in the sects and movements and other enterprises claiming to extol and teach "spirituality."

One telltale mark is where some version of the great American success ethic is manifest. Some of the so-called gospel businessmen's groups are representative of this. Their appeal is that the Lord will somehow induce material success in sales and merchandising or the like. Or, they claim, "prayer" will achieve comparable commercial dividends. One finds a plethora of similar examples among the religious telecasts. The *700-Club*—modeled after the most successful pagan TV talk show—is a seemingly endless parade of testimonies about the instantaneous rewards, of a tangible and usually material character, visited upon someone who has attained the spiritual status that the program propagates. The main emphases are upon one's effort or accomplishment and, then, the rewards promptly furnished in the form of prosperity, fame, purported healing, promotion, publicity, or whatnot. Meanwhile, there is no mention of Jesus in the wilderness episode . . . or of his repeated admonitions against notoriety and coveting notoriety, or of his poverty and the similar vocations of his disciples and the community of the Apostolic Church, or of his most ignominious execution, in a manner usually reserved for

TUESDAY AFTER THE FOURTH SUNDAY IN LENT

insurrectionists—in a manner, in other words, that was deemed a disgrace per se.

Is Jesus on the cross, in worldly terms, a success? Yet in the precincts of the famous *700-Club*, the truth about Jesus as the world's greatest failure, or about Jesus who, according to the devil, could have had it all, so far as wealth and power and success are concerned, is, simply, suppressed in favor of these vulgar stories about instant tangible success for converts.

I do not desire, in naming the *700-Club* specifically as an example of the spiritual hucksterism prevalent on television, to be critical only of that program. I cite the *700-Club* because it is the most deeply and audaciously profane of the current telecasts that I have audited. It would not surprise me to encounter something even more bold. The reason there are so many, the reason this genre of pseudo-spirituality proliferates, is, as far as I can discern, because these essentially are commercial enterprises, and merchandising organizations, having nothing to do with biblical faith or biblical spirituality. One concrete evidence of that is the fact that these success stories are presented on the program in question as if they constituted some proof of the existence and disposition, of God. That is the style of god talk distant indeed from the biblical testimonies reporting the activity of the Word of God in common history; as distant as Babel.[1]

Lord, I request, maybe even demand, answers to prayer, far too often—it is a damnable expectation of my cultural upbringing. Forgive me my expectations; place me on your clock—your calendar for me in this world, today, every day, until the Day of the Lord. Amen!

---

1. Stringfellow, *Politics of Spirituality*, 37–38.

Wednesday after the Fourth Sunday in Lent

The characteristic fact about life in the Church is worship. For the Church is now the *theatrum gloriae Dei*. The Church is the place, in the midst of ruined creation where God is glorified: where His glory is manifested, where His glory is seen. God is glorified in the Church, Christians witness to His glory, because God is the One who has no need of us yet gives us life, because He is God. Christians glorify Him because they know Him as God, and in that knowledge, they first really know themselves. The reality of worship is the manifestation of this knowledge of who God is and who men are as self. Worship is the manifestation of the relationship not only between God and men and of men to each other but of man to himself. Worship is the way restoration and reconciliation are shown forth, evidenced concretely, expressed specifically. Worship is a description of the event of restoration.

Worship, though, is not merely some re-enactment of the drama of God and men in Creation. It is the drama itself. It is the same event, not some shadow, not some facsimile, not some representation of the event. When God, therefore, is worshipped in the Church, when God is thus worshipped in history, there is taking place the focal event of history. Moreover, it is an event which breaks out of the bounds of history: worship is at once within and beyond history.

This is something of the reality of worship; and it must of course be laid alongside the practice of worship in the churches. And to do so discloses that contemporary practice conceals, often denies, and surely scandalizes the reality of worship of Almighty God. Yet where God is verily worshipped—when Christians gather as a congregation to baptize a new person or to celebrate the Lord's Supper, or to hear the Word of God—what takes place is the appropriation of things which God has made (i.e. bread, wine, water) to praise Him. What takes place is a rendering to God that which He has given to men. The appropriation in worship is focused upon the sacramental elements most specifically, perhaps, but it extends not only to bread and wine but to the building, the garments, and (most essentially) the people gathered. Everything is given to Him: everything which He first has given men. The appropriation in worship is the offering of ourselves: the offering of that which He gives in making us. *Now the very event is taking place: God reconciling men to Himself. Now prophecy is fulfilled: God is with His people. Now creation is restored: His people glorify God.*

Corporate sacramental worship is the focus of the Christian life in history, and it is the most relevant Christian witness to the world. For when God is thus worshipped, the world may see and believe. When the Church worships, God is vindicated in the midst of ruined Creation. When the Church worships, it declares the message of reconciliation (2 Corinthians 5:19). Indeed, the full dimension of the Christian life in history is worship. . . .

The sacramental dimension of corporate worship, as when a congregation celebrates Holy Communion, is the real dimension of the Christian experience of work. This is so far-reaching a distinction that it is really fitting to speak of work only as the secular experience, whereas worship describes the Christian experience. In worship, this literal worship, taking place as Christians are dispersed in the world in occupations and pursuits, the dominion of men over the rest of Creation is actually being restored.

But it is misleading to speak this of dispersed Christians, as if, in daily work, Christians are in isolation from each other in their worship, as if worship in dispersion were autonomous and individualized. There is no implication here of some notion of the invisible Church binding individual Christians in implicit fellowship while they are visibly separate in the secular world. What is the case is rather that, wherever there is a Christian, *there* is the Church in representation. It is as if the whole Church impinged upon each member. To put it otherwise, it may be said that in each Christian, in work in the world, the Church and the World confront each other. In each Christian, restored Creation and fallen creation meet, collide, come, really, into concrete and awful struggle. This is the same struggle that happens when a congregation celebrates Holy Communion in the midst of, before the eyes of, secular community. It is the struggle of the Church and World.[1]

Lord, give me the grace to be a carrier of the church as I move from worship to work; as I go from being gathered with the congregation to being thrust into the world. May my collisions be fruitful and always to your glory. Amen!

---

1. Stringfellow, "Life of Worship," 13.

Thursday after the Fourth Sunday in Lent

> ... for the Christian, vocational decision is made in conversion. To belong to Christ is to have the single, common vocation of worship. This is the life-work of Christians. Where it takes place, men are evangelized. (Precisely speaking, not evangelism but worship is our work, and evangelism is the product of worship).[1]

This is particularly pertinent for those of us in Western Christianity where, since the mid-1980s "worship evangelism" as a separate evangelism and a "purpose" for worship has been emphasized. Purpose replaced product.

> Christians, therefore, have made already the true vocational decision in conversion and are just confronted with the World's demand to make a secular vocational decision. Perhaps for some Christians the secular decision is deeply implicated, even determined, in the moment the prior decision is made. But it may be argued that it is more often the case that since God may be anywhere worshipped, since any work in the World may be sacramentalized, it is not really much of a consequence when, where, what, and even how often, a secular work-decision is made. Yet mark this, the Christian is living in the World, is meeting in the World, is confronting the World, and there is no option to make no decisions at all in the matter of secular work. Even at that, where notions of withdrawal are entertained, it is only a theoretical option; there is for Christians no such thing as withdrawal from the World. The priest, for example, does not withdraw, even though he sometimes imagines he does, from secular work. In good measure, indeed, he is in reality

---

1. Stringfellow, "Life of Worship," 17.

the secular worker maintaining the conformity of the Church to the World.

. . . One further note must be added to these comments about vocational decisions for Christians. Recall what was said earlier, that where the Christian is, dispersed in work, there is the Church, in representation. An implication for vocational decision of this is that the Church makes the decision for each Christian. Being a Christian, belonging to Christ's people, really precludes the possibility of autonomous decision in any circumstance. Perhaps Christians nowadays have little sense of their peoplehood, little sense of being the Church; but in any case, notions of individual, autonomous decision by Christians are incomprehensible in Christian faith. Where mere autonomous decision is called for from Christians . . . the erroneous attempt is made to center Christian faith upon God and the individual rather than upon God and His whole people, into which each individual is called.[2]

Concentration of thought on secular vocation thus becomes an idolatrous act and a pagan mind-set. Stringfellow is immoveable in this regard. In "An Open Letter to Jimmy Carter," in *Sojourners* magazine, he writes, "I affirm that we are called, as a vocation, to confess the active sovereignty of Jesus Christ as Lord in this world, and, in turn, to act in relation to the politics of this world in a way which honors and bespeaks the judgment of the Word of God over the politics of this world."[3]

Stringfellow believed it was pagan to declare, "Jesus is the answer," as many a bumper sticker proclaimed. He was supremely convinced that the Christian declaration to the world was, "Jesus is Lord." He was right.

---

2. Stringfellow, "Life of Worship," 17–18.
3. Stringfellow, "Open Letter to Jimmy Carter," 18.

Grant me, Lord, to have a church-wide Christian faith, that my vocation as a convert be clear, confirmed, and called into being. Though my conversion is my own, its reality in every subsequent moment belongs to the Word of God, radically active in and through the church. "One day within thy courts exceeds a thousand spent away; how happy they who keep thy law nor from thy precepts stray, for thou shalt surely bless all those who live the words they pray." Amen!

Friday after the Fourth Sunday in Lent

Stringfellow was deeply concerned by Americans' use of the Bible to justify what it, as a country, was doing either in America itself, or around the world. Israel was God's chosen nation, not America.

> My concern is to understand America biblically....
>
> The effort is to comprehend the nation, to grasp what is happening right now to the nation and to consider the destiny of the nation within the scope and style of the ethics and the ethical metaphors distinctive to the biblical witness in history.
>
> The task is to treat the nation within the tradition of biblical politics—to understand America biblically—*not* the other way around, *not* (to put it in an appropriately awkward way) to construe the Bible Americanly. There has been too much of the latter in this country's public life and religious ethos. There still is. I expect such indulgences to multiply, to reach larger absurdities, to become more scandalous, to increase blasphemously as America's crisis as a nation distends.[1] To interpret the Bible for the convenience of America, as apropos as that may seem to be to many Americans, represents a radical violence to both the character and content of the biblical message. It fosters a fatal vanity that America is a divinely favored nation and makes of it the credo of civil religion which is directly threatened by, and, hence, which is anxious and hostile toward the biblical Word. It applies them to America, so that America is conceived of as Zion: as *the* righteous nation, as people of superior political morality, as a country and society chosen and especially esteemed by God. In archetypical form in this country, material abundance, redundant productivity, technological facility, and military predominance are publicly cited to verify

---

1. Note, this was written in 1972–1973.

the alleged divine preference and prove the supposed national virtue. It is just this kind of Sadducean sophistry, distorting the biblical truth for American purposes, which, in truth, occasions the moral turmoil which the nation so manifestly suffers today and which, I believe, renders us a people as unhappy as we are hopeless. It is profane, as well as grandiose, to manipulate the Bible in order to apologize for America....

Despite the habitual malpractice of translating biblical politics as the American story, there is also the odd and contradictory custom among many Americans to denounce the truth that the Bible is political. Frequently, if incongruously, these two convictions are held concurrently by the same person, or the same sect or church or social faction. American experience as a nation—as well as biblical scholarship—discredits any attempt to Americanization of biblical politics and confounds the notion that the Bible is apolitical. What is surprising is that the latter belief persists even though so many of the biblical symbols are expressly political—*dominance, emancipation, authority, judgment, kingdom, reconciliation* among them—and even though the most familiar biblical events are notoriously political—including the drama of Israel the holy nation, the Kingdom parables in Christ's teaching, the condemnation of Christ as King of the Jews by the imperial authorities, the persecution of the apostolic congregations, the controversies between Christians and zealots, the propagation of the Book of Revelation.

Well, I do not amplify the matter here, apart from noticing that the view that the Bible is politicly neuter or innocuous—coupled, as it may be, ironically, with an American misuse of biblical politics—maintains wide currency in this nation. And this view sorely inhibits a biblical comprehension of America as a nation.[2]

Lord, in your perfections, you never change; in your work of making us like yourself, we must be changed often. May the Word of God remain active in my life to turn me as repentance requires to be facing your intentions, for my nation: your will. Amen!

2. Stringfellow, *An Ethic*, 13–15.

Saturday after the Fourth Sunday in Lent

My faith has found a resting place,
Not in device or creed;
I trust the ever-living One,
His wounds for me shall plead.

—Lidie H. Edmunds (19th century)

It is one thing to read and imbibe the Bible, it is another thing altogether to trust Jesus Christ. The fashion of the twenty-first century is to trust the Bible and make it a central point in argumentation over issues which, millennia after the record, we cannot place our finger upon for we have not any original manuscripts. Our Bible is faithful to its witness, but it is the witness, Jesus Christ, in whom we place our trust. Stringfellow encourages us here.

> I am not one inclined toward using the conditioning of history to explain away discrepancy or incongruity in the Bible. At the same time, I harbor no compulsion to neatly harmonize scripture. . . . The whole notion that the Bible must be homogenized or rendered consistent is a common academic imposition upon biblical literature, but it often ends in an attempt to ideologize the Bible in a manner which denies the most elementary truth of the biblical witness, namely, that it bespeaks the dynamic and viable participation of the word of God in the common events of this world.
>
> The militant character of the Word of God in history refutes any canon of mere consistency in the biblical witness. To read the Bible is to hear of and behold events in which the word of God is concerned, attended by the particularity and, to human beings, the ambiguity of actual happenings. Any efforts to read the Bible as a

treatise abstractly constructed or conformed usurps the genius of the Bible as testament of the word of God active in history. If the biblical witness were internally strictly consonant, after the modes of ideology or philosophy, the mystery of revelation in this world would be abolished; revelation itself would be categorically precluded.

What is to be expected, instead of simplistic consistency, in listening to the Bible, allowing for vagaries and other limitations of human insight, is *coherence:* a basic integrity of the word of God or the fidelity of the personality of God in his creation.

I do not mean to extol inconsistency. I am glad enough to find one text of the Bible which seems, to my mind, in obvious harmony with another passage, but I do mean to caution against making a rubric of consistency that violates the most essential characteristic of the biblical witness and which, usually nourishes vanity in reading and using the Bible, and which, invariably, issues in manipulation, or oversight, or suppression of some dimensions of the Bible.[1]

The ideologized Bible becomes the Bible idolized, and we have been confronted with this for decades. The Scriptures themselves warn of the precipitous nature of worshipping idols. This Lenten time should exist to help us "*turn from idols and worship the living God.*"

Lord, help me discern when I am elevating the Bible above its rightful place as a testament to you. May any idol, including an idolized Bible, be anathema to me, and might I commit to trust which is found only in Jesus Christ. Amen!

---

1. Stringfellow, "Bible and Ideology."

Monday after the Fifth Sunday in Lent

The revelation of the word of God is, always, more manifold and more versatile than human comprehension. What I anticipate in the biblical witness is not consistency so much as coherence. I can live and act as a biblical person without the former, but without the latter I cannot live.

So in the Bible I look for style, not stereotype, for precedent, not model, for parable, not proposition, for analogue not aphorism, for paradox, not syllogism, for signs, not statutes. The encounter with the biblical witness is empirical, as distinguished from scholastic, and it is confessional, rather than literalistic; in either case, it, over and above any consideration, involves the common reader in affirming the historicity of the word of God throughout the present age, in the biblical era as such, and imminently as well.

My esteem for the biblical witness and my approach to the Bible should be enough to disclose my skepticism about current efforts to construct political theology according to some ideological model. . . . Even the most venerable identification of the biblical witness for the oppressed and dispossessed of this age does not render the biblical people ideologically captivated. The effort to distinguish a biblical apologetic for Marxism (remember this is written in 1976) is no different from those which have sought to theologize capitalism, colonialism, war and profligate consumption. Whatever the subject ideology or policy, attempts such as these trivialize the Bible.

In other words, biblical politic *never* implies a particular, elaborated political theology, whether it be one echoing the status quo or one which aspires to overthrow the status quo. The gospel is not ideology and, categorically, the gospel cannot be ideologized. Biblical politics always has a posture in tension and opposition to the prevalent system, and to any prospective or incipient status quo, and to the ideologies of either regime or revolution. Biblical politics are alienated from the politics of this age.

Let no one read into these remarks gratuitous comfort for simplistic and unresponsive answers to political issues of enormous complexity, such as all the nations suffer, after the manner of those who incant the name of Jesus superstitiously. It is literally pagan, i.e., unbiblical to recite, "Jesus is the answer." The Bible is more definitive: the biblical affirmation is "Jesus is Lord." The Bible makes a political statement of the reign of Christ preempting all the rulers, and all pretenders to the thrones and dominions, subjecting incumbents and revolutionaries, surpassing the doctrines and promises of the ideologies of this world . . . "the Lordship of Jesus Christ in this age means a resilient and tireless witness to confound, rebuke and undo every regime, and every potential regime, unto the moment when humankind is accounted over the nations, ideologies, and other principalities in the last judgment of the word of God."[1]

Lord God, you are over and above all we can devise or dream of; you are Lord of all and the implications are vast. Keep me from being satisfied with you being "the answer," and continue to show me what your Lordship expects of me. Amen!

---

1. Stringfellow, "Bible and Ideology," 18.

Tuesday after the Fifth Sunday in Lent

I do not pray for these only, but for those who are to believe in me through their word, that they may all be one; even as thou, Father, art in me, and I in thee, that they also may be in us, so that the world may believe that thou hast sent me.

—John 17:20–21

The unity of the Church is a *gift*, not something sought or grasped or attained, but, as with any gift, something which may be refused or dishonored or misused. . . .

The unity given to the Church at Pentecost is vouchsafed for all men baptized into the Body of Christ since Pentecost. It is this same unity received and enjoyed within the Church among the members of the Church and manifested and verified in the life of the Church in the world which *is* the witness of the Church to the world . . . the unity of the Church is given to be the content and shape of the Church's love for and service to the world.

Nor does God give unity to the Church for His own sake, as if He needed anything at all, even the unity of those who call upon His name. The gift of unity is not an act of necessity for God, but an act of generosity of God.

It is for the sake of the world, for the sake of all persons and powers who do not or will not call upon God's name, that unity is given to the Church, for it is in the unity of the Church that the world may behold the unity into which God invites the whole of the world. . . .

Hence the very unity of the Church is the authentic witness of the Church.

Where the Church denies or rejects or perverts the gift of unity the witness to the world is lost. That is a loss the Church suffers even more acutely than the world, though it must be remembered that God thereby suffers no loss whatsoever. The disunity of the Church does not stop God's love for the world, nor does the disunity of the Church modify or diminish God's witness to Himself. The disunity of the Church, rather, deprives the Church of the joy of witnessing to God's care for and work in the world. . . .

The recovery of unity . . . does essentially involve the establishment and existence of the Church as a living people, a holy nation, manifest and militant, in this world, which embraces as its witness to a broken, divided, and fallen world all diversities of mankind and which empirically transcends here and now and already all that separates, alienates, and segregates men from themselves, each other, and the rest of creation . . . unity is integral to witness; the Church exists merely for the sake of the world . . . the witness requires a unity encompassing *all* diversities of human life. But that unity does inherent a total community and organic union of all who are baptized professing the same Biblical and Apostolic faith, living in communion with one another now, and with the whole of the people of God who have gone before and who are yet to be, and sharing a manifold but common ministry for the world.

The ecclesiology and polity of the total community of the Church are not matters of indifference or unimportance, but they are secondary and auxiliary to the unity of the actual common life of the Church. The style of the common life of the Church and of the members of the Church is most manifest and most comprehensive in the sacraments given and ordained by Christ Himself: in baptism and in the holy communion. There can be no unity which is witness unless there be a common understanding and universal recognition, within the whole Church, of the baptism of each member of the Church. Nor can there be such a unity of the Church lest all and any who are baptized be welcome into the common life of the Church which is the holy communion.

Both baptism and the holy communion are ecumenical sacraments in the broadest meaning of ecumenical, that is, both are sacraments of the unity of all mankind in Christ.[1]

1. Stringfellow, "Unity of the Church," 394–400.

So often, Lord Christ, I "go to church" for me—intentionally for me and not for others and certainly not for the world. Change my intent—I will it—that intentionally I will be part of the church for the sake of its unity and therefore for the sake of, and witness to, the world. Amen.

Wednesday after the Fifth Sunday in Lent

Baptism and the holy communion—far from being mere esoteric religious rituals—are most concretely political and social in character. Baptism confesses faith and experience of the Church, and of the people of the Church, in all times and places in the grace of God in Christ reconciling the whole world including, now, this particular person being baptized and marks the initiation and guarantee of the new life of the one baptized, in this world in the society of the Church. Holy Communion is the characteristic form of the new life given to men in this world as the society of the Church and at once recalls and re-presents and enacts the whole history of God's grace in the world from the beginning of the world, and anticipates and calls for and expects the consummation of the work of God's grace in the end of the world, and celebrates and enjoys and relies upon the vitality of God's grace in the world, here and now, in the present age between Creation and the Eschaton. Let it be emphasized that the holy communion is not a celebration of God's presence in any sanctuary or shrine, but it is the celebration of God's presence and activity in the world and those who gather now and then in a sanctuary of the Church do so as a witness to the world that God's presence and action in the world is truly reconciling since those who gather have been and are in fact already reconciled, despite their sin, despite any affliction common to men, despite even the power of death itself, despite everything known and suffered in this world by men.

Unity as witness requires a recovery in the presently separated churches of the sacramental integrity of both baptism and the holy communion, and that may too easily imply that, since the validity of baptism in most denominations and even sects is already generally acknowledged in the several churches, the main course to unity is inter-communion. . . .

While inter-communion between churches in different places is a step toward unity which is witness, inter-communion without organic union among churches in the same place would, I suggest, further confuse the witness of the Church . . . any unity is too cheap which merely represents a formal theological entente or an abstract reciprocity respecting baptism and the communion, without a resolution in the organic union of the Church of all secular divisions of the several churches. . . .

Unity means not just friendly relations and fraternal collaborations—nor even intercommunion—among the several church of Protestantism, Orthodoxy, Anglicanism, and Rome, as welcome as that may be, but in the end it means the organic union of all the churches for the sake of the world. . . .

The unity of the Church which is witness to the world is a gift of God in Pentecost. As the account relates (Acts 2) in Pentecost is God filling the Apostles with His Holy Spirit in a way which shows on-lookers and strangers the universality of the Word of God, in a way which discloses that the Word of God is addressed to all men in all times in all the world, in a way, in other words, in which it is clear that the Word of God is present and active in this world and accessible to every man whoever he be, wherever he be, in a way, indeed, in which the on-looker is converted . . . the gift of unity . . . is versatile enough to reach and embrace all men in all of their diversities and divisions and separations. Pentecost is, remember a public *witness* to the Word of God.[1]

How often I have considered the personal applications of Pentecost and omitted from my conscious mind its public witness. Lord Jesus, grant me grace to see the necessity of unity as public witness of the church, and the filling of the Holy Spirit as the enablement of being a part of that witness. Amen.

1. Stringfellow, "Unity of the Church," 394–400.

Thursday after the Fifth Sunday in Lent

What is the meaning of God having concern for the poor of the world?

The Word of God is secretly present in the life of the poor, as in the life of the whole world, but most of the poor do not know the Word of God. These two facts constitute the dialectic of the Church's mission among the poor. All that is required for the mission of the Church in Harlem [editor's note: or any other city] is there already, save one thing: the presence of the community which has and exercises the power to discern the presence of the Word of God in the ordinary life of the poor as it is lived every day. What is the requisite mission, to the exposure of God's Word within the precarious and perishing existence of poverty, is the congregation which relies on and celebrates the resurrection. That which is essential for mission is confession of the faith—immediately, notoriously, and in whatever terms or symbols or actions are indigenous to the moment and place.

The characteristic of the life of God which the Church needs most to recall nowadays, I think, is how absurdly simple His action in the world already makes our witness to Him in the world.

The churches have been beset by a false notion of charity. They have supposed that the inner city must become much like the outer city before the Gospel can be heard. They have thought that mission follows charity. They have favored crusades and abandoned mission. I am all for changing the face of Harlem, but the mission of the Church depends not on social reformation in the neighborhood, as desperately as that is needed, but upon the presence of the Word of God in the society of the poor as it is right now. If the mere Gospel is not a whole salvation for the most afflicted men, it is no comfort to other men in less affliction. Mission does *not* follow charity; faith does *not* follow works, either for donor or recipient. On the contrary, mission is *itself* the only charity which Christians have to offer to the poor, the only work which Christians have to do.

The premise of most urban church work, it seems, is that in order for the Church to minister among the poor, the church has to be rich, that is, to have specially trained personnel, huge funds, and many facilities, rummage to distribute, and a whole battery of social services. Just the opposite is the case. The Church must be free to be poor in order to minister among the poor. The Church must trust the Gospel enough to come among the poor with nothing to offer the poor except the Gospel, except the power to apprehend and the courage to reveal the Word of God as it is already mediated in the life of the poor.

When the Church has the freedom itself to be poor among the poor, it will know how to use what riches it has. When the Church has that freedom, it will be a missionary people again in all the world.[1]

Make me to understand the real meaning of "poor," then take me as I now am and make me poor so as to minister among the poor. I am willing for my wealth to be used among the poor for their care, no matter what my wealth may be. Amen.

---

1. Stringfellow, *My People Is the Enemy*, 98–99.

Friday after the Fifth Sunday in Lent

The biblical witness is a living one encompassing as much diversity among biblical people as the Holy Spirit engenders, and biblical theology is never quite settled or completed, never stereotyped or platitudinous, but is constantly dynamic and insightful as it yields to the militancy of the action of the Word of God in common history.

The resilient and historic character of the biblical witness—one might call it the existential integrity of that witness—has nowhere been more apparent than in politics. The New Testament itself verifies that in the contrasts to be found in Romans 13 as compared to Revelation 13, to cite one example. As the biblical witness has continued since the New Testament era, similar contrasts have been redundant, not only as between the experience of the church before and after the Constantinian arrangement, but also in the confrontation between biblical people and a great variety of regimes within the periods both prior to and subsequent to the Constantinian establishment. The situation is typified, to a degree which is often confusing, in the pluralism of Christendom in America. Yet, if that be the fact, in the present American circumstances, it must not be exploited to dilute or equivocate the biblical witness in America, and it must not be the pretext for suppressing or silencing the tension which inheres between gospel and politics. . . .

I affirm that we are called, as a vocation, to confess the active sovereignty of Jesus Christ as Lord in this world, and, in turn, to act in relation to the politics of this world in a way which honors and bespeaks the judgment of the Word of God over the politics of this world. . . .

I fear that the political truth about America is that since the time of the Second World War—since technology superseded industrialization as the dominant institutional and ideological power in society—the nation has been suffering a counter-revolution. Its conspicuous feature has been the proliferation of extra-constitutional agencies and authorities which, in their political impact, have become the effectual regime of the nation, displacing the inherited governmental institutions, usurping the rule of law, and investing ruling authority beyond accountability to human beings....

The issue, politically and theologically, which has to be confronted concerns the entrenchment of lawless—and predatory—authority. It has to do with vesting of the demonic institutionally in the principalities and powers of a technocratic society.[1]

Jesus did not live in a technological society, however, he lived in a politically intricate society where the "elite" of the Jews were in a ruling authority beyond their ordained purpose which placed them "beyond accountability" to anyone—hence they could, and did, form a demonic alliance with Herod and Pontius Pilate. The agency was, for Jesus, deadly. Lies, manipulation, tepidness, superciliousness each played their part in Jesus unlawful death. The warnings are dire. Stringfellow concludes brilliantly as we approach the illegalities of Holy Week: "Deception is more humiliating than rejection. Exploitation is more inhuman than exclusion. Indifference is more embittering than hostility. Condescension is more provocative than hate."[2]

Lord Jesus Christ, the serpentine methods of principalities and powers confuse the mind, dishearten the spirit, and disturb the soul. What was done to Jesus is being done to his people around the world. Keep me aware. Keep me in prayer. Make me a clear biblical witness. Amen!

1. Stringfellow, "Open Letter to Jimmy Carter," 23.
2. Stringfellow, *My People Is the Enemy*, 103.

Saturday after the Fifth Sunday in Lent

Tomorrow is Palm Sunday—many see it as a victory parade when in reality, it is a death march. Thinking they were arriving, the many did not begin to realize what was merely beginning. Their justification was not yet being experienced, for they were not aware fully of their need for justice and justification. Then there is Jesus, himself who teaches his followers that just being who they are in their integrity is their service of worship. Everything was being put up front for victory was sure—they were betting on it. But not to get ahead of ourselves, victory is not the same thing as worship. Remember Jesus enters the temple and finds money changers, but money nonetheless.

> In worship, men offer themselves and all of their decisions, actions, and words to God, it is well that they use their money as the witness of that offering. Money is, thus, used sacramentally within the Church and not contributed as to some charity or given because the Church, as such, has any need for money.
>
> The sacramental use of money in the formal and gathered worship of the Church is authenticated—as are all other churchly sacramental practices—in the sacramental use of money in the common life of the world.
>
> No end of ways exist in which money can be so appropriated and spent, but, whatever the concrete circumstances, the consistent mark of such a commitment of money is a person's freedom from the idolatry of money. . . .
>
> The charity of Christians, in other words, in the use of money sacramentally—in both the liturgy and in the world—has no serious similarity to conventional charity but is always a specific dramatization of the members of the Body of Christ losing their life in order that the world be given life. For a member of the Church, therefore, it

always implies a particular confession that his money is not his own because his life is not his own, but, by the example of God's own love, belongs to the world.

That one's own life belongs to the world, that one's money and possessions, talents and time, influence and health, all belong to the whole world is, I trust, why the saints are habitués of poverty and ministers to the outcasts, friends of the humiliated and, commonly, unpopular themselves. Contrary to many legends, the saints are not spooky figures, morally superior, abstentious, pietistic. They are seldom even remembered, much less haloed. In truth, all men are called to be saints, but that just means called to be fully human, to be perfect—that is, whole, mature, fulfilled. The saints are simply those men and women who relish the event of life as a gift and who realize that the only way to honor such a gift is to give it away.

No doubt some will think all this imprudent and impractical, and, in any event, difficult to practice and apt to be unpopular. But the answer to that is that fidelity to the Gospel is not measured by the affluence of the Church but rather by how the Church loves and serves the world in deploying and spending the wealth the Church happens at a certain time to have to give. And, for an individual Christian, the answer to that is that though money be a beguiling idol and one which is easy to reverence, money has yet to justify a single human being or secure for him the freedom to be a person, while there are many men, who, having feared that money or other property is God, have found it worthless except as evidence against themselves.[1]

I thought you needed my money, Lord Jesus, when it appears you needed, or at least wanted, me. Money figures much into the days from Palm Sunday through the death of Judas. Keep me from thinking victory leads to wealth. The wealth of betrayal calls for serious repentance. Amen!

---

1. Stringfellow, *Dissenter in a Great Society*, 46–47.

Monday in Holy Week

Christians are, nowadays, so accustomed to esteeming the disciples as exemplary in faith that it seems a surprise to notice that the New Testament Gospel accounts do not report any of the disciples as believers....

The truth, poignant as it may be, is that the disciples were profoundly skeptical about Jesus. In their experience of his ministry they were variously enthralled, mystified, bemused, apprehensive, confounded, disillusioned. During Holy Week, their elation on Palm Sunday very quickly turned into consternation; by Good Friday very quickly they have become fearful and hysterical; by Easter they are both embittered and bereft. And through all of it they remain steadfast in their disbelief.

If for us, the disciples can be said to exemplify anything, then they must be said to exemplify not faith, but incredulity. This represents, I suggest, the most significant identification of the disciples with contemporary Christians. If any of us are to claim a biblical attitude of faith in Christ, it is necessary first of all to cope with the exemplary disbelief of the disciples....

The Gospels are redundant in verifying the reality—one might also say, the veracity—of the skepticism of the disciples about Jesus Christ as Lord. When, for instance, Jesus asks them, "Who do you say that I am?" the true response of Peter is found not in his impulsive reply, "You are the Christ, the Son of the living God," but in the reaction of that confession, after Jesus began to show his disciples that he must suffer many things, be killed, and on the third day, be raised (Matthew 16:13–21). Confronted with this version of the vocation of the Christ, Peter exclaims, "God forbid, Lord! This shall never happen to you" (Matthew 16:22–23). Thus Peter rehearses himself for Good Friday (Mark 14:66–72)....

And, typically, the disciples are reported to be astonished by his parables; at times they protest that he teaches in parables, and sometimes they seek from Jesus private explanations of parables (Matthew 13:36–51; 13:10–17).... Throughout their whole experience with Jesus in Holy Week as well as earlier, the disciples are found misconstruing his authority, or doubting it, or, sometimes, opposing it....

This should be enough to render people wary of huckster preachers or celebrity evangelists who assert that more intimacy with Jesus of an intense, private, or exclusive nature is faith. This is a fascinating, tempting, simplistic, but unbiblical doctrine, and multitudes are seduced by it into fancying that to be, somehow, in the presence of Jesus is so compelling and so positive an experience that doubt of all sorts is dispelled quickly, conclusively, as if magically.... But according to the New Testament, the disbelief lingers, admixed with hurt and bewilderment, in the immediate aftermath of the resurrection....

If the authorities of this world—including the whole diverse array of principalities and powers, ecclesial, political, military, commercial—recognize Jesus as Christ the Lord, it is because his reign is active now and constantly disrupts and confounds their rule and exposes their power, which is no more than the sanction of death, as transient and fraudulent....

The kingdom of which Christ is Lord is not worldly but it is not otherworldly; for it is a kingdom in this world, an historical and political reality, which both devastates and consummates the apparently prevailing order and all of its regimes and putative regimes or revolutionary causes. The life to which those in Christ are called consists of living as a society, now under the reign of the Word of God, beholden to Christ as Lord of all life within the whole of creation, until that day when his reign is vindicated and the fulness of the power of death is exhausted, and all persons, principalities, and powers are rendered accountable and this history ends.

So I have not offered any of these remarks with intent to be harsh on the disciples, for I remember that on

Maundy Thursday Jesus promises the disciples that they will be made sufficient in the Word of God to be witnesses to Christ's reign throughout the world (John 14). That same promise is ratified when Jesus, risen, appears to the disciples (Luke 24:44–49). On the day of Pentecost that promise is fulfilled and it is attested in Acts that the disciples become worthy of the promise.[1]

Lord, I believe but I need help with unbelief on so many occasions. So help me as you helped your average disciple to trust your heart, your promise, when we cannot either see or read your stated purpose. Amen!

---

1. Stringfellow, "Exemplary Disbelief," 33–38.

Tuesday in Holy Week

Jesus has but three more days to live prior to crucifixion. The awfulness of human sin is coalescing with Jesus, himself, as the cosmic focal point.

> [A] startling omission in "spirituality" quarters . . . is mention of the fall and the significance of the fall. To be sure, in . . . personal anecdotes . . . there will almost invariably be a recitation of private sin, predictably implicating one or another of the conventional vices or prosaic lusts—sex, booze, drugs, etc., etc. Such matters are encompassed within the purview of the fall. But the fall means far more than that. The fall refers to the profound disorientation, affecting all relationships in the totality of creation, concerning identity, place, connection, purpose, vocation. The subject of the fall is not only in the personal realm, in the sense of you or me, but the whole creation and each and every item of created life. The fall means the reign of chaos throughout the creation now, so that even that which is ordained by the ruling powers as "order" is in truth, chaotic. The fall means a remarkable confusion which all beings—principalities as well as persons—suffer as to who they are and why they exist. The fall means the consignment of all created life, and of the realm of time, to the power of death.
>
> To understate or otherwise diminish the reality of the fall radically distorts not only the corpus of the confession of biblical faith but also the comprehension of biblical folk of the world as it is and of that which is involved in the redemption of the world. Suffice it here to say that the biblical description of the fall liberates people to view this world with unflinching, resistant realism. That is part of the ethos in which the judgment of the Word of God takes place. At the same time, that same realism is an indisputable credential for witness and ministry, for any ministry

at all. And, perhaps most urgent, that same realism, with which, as Ephesians might say, the saints are equipped in their understanding of the fall, is the very threshold of hope. It is, to notice another irony, that which enables living in this world in hope.

What I am saying, of course, in part, is that much of what is asserted to be "spirituality" is utterly alien to biblical spirituality and is, in truth, no more than nihilism. It is a form of idolatry of death and sometimes, more particularly, an idolatry of the fear of death. In any case, it is a worship of nothing—a fascination with no thing, a heavily conditioned self-conscious, circular pursuit of nothing, an elevation of nonexistence, a truly and appropriately chaotic endeavor, a glorification, finally, of the genius of the power of death. Among the most widespread symptoms of this morbid effort are the frantic preoccupations—endemic now in American culture—with security and survival. More often than not these manifestations are exposed as nihilistic because they are accompanied by defamation and persecution of the underclasses of society; notably the dispossessed and the homeless.

Nihilism offers no hope for living, but it contrives some substitutes for hope. Perhaps the most familiar is hedonism. In place of hope there is immediate gratification, usually sensual or material, and commonly in gross proportions far beyond immediate human needs. That is one reason why gluttony has become a prime social and personal problem in this culture, even though the churches seem steadfast in their apathy about it, and the ruling economic, commercial, and political powers seem equally determined to encourage and increase gluttony as if it were some civic virtue.

Nihilism is, at the same time, a frequent sponsor of nostalgia as a substitute for hope. This is a heavy commercial fad. It may bear little or no correspondence to the historic truth, but it serves to fill the void where ideology articulates no hope and it condones carrying nostalgia into fantasy dimensions.

Such devices and deceptions as these abet the insulation of people from the realism of living in the midst of the fall with some sense of humanity, for themselves and in relationships. Then, after a while, the humanizing faculties malfunction and fail; they become so suppressed or neglected as gifts of life that they atrophy. And so it seems that nihilism signifies a triumph of death over life, spreading its own idolatry.[1]

It is for this cause we must not make of the Passion of Christ a nostalgic or romanticized history—it is realism or it becomes nothing.

Lord Jesus Christ, "The Old Rugged Cross" may bring back memories but it doesn't bring back the reality of the Roman crucifixion tool. The barbaric nature of Jesus' death is not able to be translated into safe and easy thoughts or language. Keep me from trying. Give it to me straight, no ice, not stirred or shaken. Let the Truth shake me. Amen!

---

1. Stringfellow, *Politics of Spirituality*, 38–40.

Wednesday in Holy Week

The regimes of much professed contemporary spirituality or those of various brands of pseudo-spirituality dwell upon self-denial or self-suppression as a basic secret for attaining the state of selfhood sought through a particular "spiritual" practice. Within the churches, preachers are notorious in spreading the impression that some such experience of self-denial is requisite in gaining spiritual status. When pressed for specifics about such supposed chastenings, these same preachers, in my observation, are seldom able to go beyond an advocacy of surrendering bad habits, usually related to one or another of the common appetites. I hear little from these same quarters about repentance or renewal of persons or restoral of life. That comes as no special surprise, since the whole notion of self-denial or suppression of self, associated with a purported spirituality, is really a matter of self-indulgence, a vainglorious idea, a superficial "spiritual" exercise at most.

I reiterate what has heretofore been affirmed—in this book—and will again and again be affirmed—in this book: Holiness is not an attainment, in any sense of the term, but is a gift of the Word of God. Holiness is not a badge of achievement for a saint but is wrought in the life, in the very being, of an ordinary person by the will of the Word of God. Holiness, from the vantage point of the person who may truthfully be said to be holy, is, in the most elementary meaning, the restoration of integrity and wholeness to a person. That inherently involves, for that person, repentance—utter repentance, encompassing and comprehending the whole of that person's existence, even recollecting one's creation in the Word of God by the Word of God. It involves, as well, a prospective or continued living in repentance unto the very day of the Judgment of the Word of God in the consummation of the history of the world. But such radical repentance does not imply, much less require, self-denial and any sort of suppression or sublimation of self. Quite the contrary: In becoming and being sanctified, *every* facet, feature, attribute, and detail of a person is exposed and rejuvenated, rendered new as if in its original condition again, and restored. Thus, instead of self-denial, what is taking place is more nearly the opposite of self-denial: in place of denial there is fulfillment.

The experience of Saint Paul is edifying in this respect, particularly since Paul has furnished us with more news of his experience in becoming and being a saint than any other New Testament character. To take a straightforward example, Paul in his early career boasted that he was the most zealous of those who persecuted the Gospel and confessors of the Gospel. From that we know that Paul had a quality, perchance even talent, which is described as *zeal*. Later on, Paul becomes the most zealous apologist for the Gospel, even aspiring to confront the Emperor with his advocacy. Lo! Paul retains this quality of zeal, save now, when he has become the great apologist, this aspect of his personhood is turned around, renewed, matured, restored to him in something like its original integrity in his own creation in the Word of God. The zeal of Paul does not have to be excised in order for him to become and be a saint, although he had engaged in this zeal of his to harass and harm and inhibit the Gospel. Had his zeal been somehow suppressed or extinguished, it would then have been less than the person Paul implicated in conversion and in becoming holy. And *that* becomes a self-contradiction: It is only the whole person, fully repentant, without anything withheld, denied, secreted, who can be holy.[1]

Lord Christ, "I will not be denied," according to a hymnwriter of the previous century; I will not be denied my self or my Savior—both are involved in the integrity of salvation and of the one saved. I am, precisely because he also is "I Am." Amen!

1. Stringfellow, *Politics of Spirituality*, 41–42.

Maundy Thursday

Jesus, knowing denial, destitution, demonism, and death are each in agreement with the other to take him down . . . down to death, even to the very pit of hell. What does Jesus do in the impending political charade set in motion by Judas? He feeds his disciples, including Judas, a supper—a supper wrought with meaning, mourning, and yet hope. But death is at the door.

> One does not have to believe in an anthropomorphic idea of a devil with horns and a tail and a red complexion to admit, understand and reconcile with any other realities of contemporary life, the vitality of the power of death in history . . . in this fallen world as men know it in their ordinary lives, in this world with all of its principalities and powers, the ascendant reality, apart from the reality of God himself, is death.[1]

> Loneliness is the specific apprehension of a person of his own death in relation to the impending death of all men and all things. . . . Loneliness . . . is the ordinary but still overwhelming anxiety that all relationships are lost. . . . Loneliness is the most traumatic, drastic, fundamental repudiation of God. Loneliness is the most elementary expression of original sin.
> There is no man who does not know loneliness—yet there is no man who is alone.[2]

Later this same evening, Jesus will begin to experience loneliness when he asks the disciples why they could not remain awake one hour to pray with him—he was foreseeing his hour on the

---

1. Stringfellow, *Conscience and Obedience*, 69.
2. Stringfellow, *Instead of Death*, 15.

Roman killing machine. And this anticipation of death by political decree and cowardice, left Jesus a lonely man.

> The biblical topic is politics. The Bible is about the politics of fallen creation and the politics of redemption; the politics of all nations, institutions, ideologies, and causes of the world and the politics of the Kingdom of God; the politics of Babylon and the politics of Jerusalem; the politics of the Antichrist; and the politics of Jesus Christ; the politics of the demonic powers and principalities and the politics of the timely judgment of God as sovereign; the politics of death and the politics of life; apocalyptic politics and eschatological politics.
>
> Throughout the diversity of the biblical saga as history and as literature, the priority of politics remains prominent. The Bible expounds with extraordinary versatility, now one way and then another, and another, the singular issue of salvation—which is to say, the preemptive *political* issue. It bespeaks the reality of human life consummated in society within time in this world, now and here, as the promise of renewal and fulfillment vouchsafed for all humans and for every nation—for the whole of Creation—throughout time.[3]

Jesus faces the politics of elite Judaism in concert with no-life Roman puppets assigned to a far end of the empire. Together they scheme to arrest the rabble-rouser in the cover of darkness. These represent what has become the "established order" for Judea—and Jesus, among thousands, will suffer at their political corruption and incompetencies.

> It goes without saying in my view, that in circumstances where moral decadence in the sense meant here becomes so pervasive in a nation, one can discern and identify maturity, conscience, and paradoxically, freedom in human beings *only* among those who are in conflict with the established order—those who are opponents of the status quo, those in rebellion against the system, those who are prisoners, resisters, fugitives, and victims. And

---

3. Stringfellow, *Ethic for Christians*, 14–15.

only, by the same token, incidentally, can one postulate any ground of hope for a viable future.[4]

Lord Jesus Christ, you knew all along the consequences of the gospel proclamation—that men and women do not take kindly to grace when life has always been meritorious. Deliver me to a Maundy Thursday worldview which abandons me completely and maturely to hope. Amen.

---

4. Stringfellow, *Ethic for Christians*, 31.

Good Friday

> Christ suffered loneliness without despair. In the radical loneliness of Christ is the assurance that no man is alone.
> In surrender to death, in hell, in the event which the presence and power of death is most notorious, undisguised, militant and pervasive, the reality and Grace of God are triumphant.[1]

Triumph in death, one of the extraordinary ironies of the Word of God . . . of the gospel itself. Such realities dare not be missed in our Good Friday liturgies.

> I have found that my own anxieties always contain the knowledge, the triumph, and the enjoyment of God. "He descended into Hell." That is very cheerful news. There is nothing less than Hell unknown to Him. There is nothing I have known this side of Hell that is unfamiliar to Him. There is nothing known to me which I am wont to call Hell which He has not already known. Nor is there anything beyond these realms which, even though unknown to me, He does not know. Anxieties, therefore, are not unwelcomed in my life or in my household, since anxieties do not end in themselves as the psychiatrists assert.[2]

Good Friday should be the ultimate in anxiety—in grief—in mourning—in everything ending in a *"chronos"*—defined moment (*"chronos"* = chronology or having to do with the end of time as differing from telos = ending of purpose). Anything of value seems in Calvary and the stone-cold tomb to announce its end—terminated—over—never again to be heard of. Tomorrow is not

---

1. Stringfellow, *Instead of Death*, 21.
2. Stringfellow, *Private and Public Faith*, 63–64.

promised, so it appears. But, Stringfellow hits a high point in his insights with the following words:

> I understand grief to be the total experience of loss, anger, outrage, fear, regret, melancholy, abandonment, temptation, bereftness, helplessness suffered privately, within one's self, in response to the happening of death. By distinction and contrast, I comprehend mourning as the liturgies of recollection, memorial, affection, honor, gratitude, confession, empathy, intercession, meditation, anticipation for the life of the one who is dead. Empirically, in the reality of someone's death, and in the aftermath of it, grief and mourning are, of course, jumbled. It is, I think, part of the healing of mourning to sort out and identify the one from the other. In any case, of all those I have known and loved and grieved and mourned, Anthony's life was the closest to my own and the most complementary, so his death is, my most intimate experience—so far—what I have to say is: grieving is about weeping, and wailing, and gnashing of teeth; mourning is about rejoicing—rejoicing in the Lord. From that standpoint, I confess I have found mourning Anthony and exquisite, bittersweet, experience. I enjoy mourning Anthony.[3]

As Stringfellow mourns, enjoys mourning his close friend, Anthony, we can mourn Jesus Christ, for "we do not grieve as those who have no hope."

A commitment to and an enjoyment of mourning is what I need about now in this Lent. Grant such a vision of the Word of God that I will know I am never left alone by you, Lord Christ, and that any who have left already are a part of the great company of saints, and they include me, so I am never alone. Amen!

---

3. Stringfellow, "Life of Worship," 11–16.

Bibliography

Stringfellow, William. "The Bible and Ideology." *Sojourners*, September 1966.
———. *Conscience and Obedience: The Politics of Romans 13 and Revelation 13 in Light of the Second Coming*. Waco, TX: Word, 1977.
———. *Count It All Joy: Reflections on Faith, Doubt, and Temptation Seen through the Letter of James*. Grand Rapids: Eerdmans, 1967.
———. "The Crisis Accepted." In *Youth in Crisis: The Responsibility of the Schools*, edited by Peter C. Moore, 35–42. New York: Seabury, 1966.
———. *Dissenter in a Great Society: A Christian View of America in Crisis*. New York: Holt, Rinehart, and Winston, 1966.
———. *An Ethic for Christians & Other Aliens in a Strange Land*. Waco, TX: Word, 1973.
———. "Exemplary Disbelief." *Sojourners*, March 1980.
———. *Free in Obedience*. New York: Seabury, 1964.
———. *Instead of Death*. New York: Seabury, 1976.
———. "The Life of Worship and the Legal Profession." Faculty Papers, 3rd series. National Council, 1956.
———. "Living with Defeat." *Witness*, May 1977.
———. *My People Is the Enemy: An Autobiographical Polemic*. New York: Holt, Rinehart, and Winston, 1964.
———. "An Open Letter to Jimmy Carter." *Sojourners*, October 1976.
———. *The Politics of Spirituality*. Philadelphia: Westminster, 1984.
———. *A Private and Public Faith*. Grand Rapids: Eerdmans, 1962.
———. *A Second Birthday: A Personal Confrontation with Illness, Pain, and Death*. Garden City: Doubleday, 1970.
———. *A Simplicity of Faith: My Experience in Mourning*. Nashville: Abingdon, 1983.
———. "Through Dooms of Love." In *New Theology, No. 2*, edited by Martin Marty and Dean Peerman, 294–95. New York: MacMillan, 1965.
———. "The Unity of the Church as a Witness of the Church." *Anglican Theological Review* 100 (2018) 523–30.

www.ingramcontent.com/pod-product-compliance
Lightning Source LLC
Chambersburg PA
CBHW072009090426
42734CB00033B/2322